MANAGING WITH PASSION

MANAGING WITH PASSION

MAKING THE MOST OF YOUR JOB AND YOUR LIFE

SIGMUND G. GINSBURG

John Wiley & Sons, Inc.

New York • Chichester • Brisbane • Toronto • Singapore

ISBN 0-471-14558-0 (paper)

Printed in the United States of America

10 9 8 7 6 5 4 3 2 1

In memory of my father, Saul Ginsburg

ACKNOWLEDGMENTS

I have been fortunate over the past thirty-two years that my bosses, Harvey Sherman, Timothy W. Costello, Henry R. Winkler, and Ellen V. Futter have been individuals whom I greatly respected and liked. They have been wise counselors and friends, colleagues, mentors, and role models, and I am very grateful to them. I am also grateful to my colleagues at all levels in the organizations in which I have worked who have shared the challenges and joys of management with me. I appreciate the guidance and assistance provided by Robert L. Bernstein and the encouragement and efforts of my editor Janet Coleman, the many individuals at John Wiley & Sons, and Nancy Marcus Land at Publications Development Company who made this book a reality. There is indeed more to life than work and I am grateful beyond words for the support and joy provided by my family, Rose, Judith, Beth, David, Simon, Naomi, and Marty.

PREFACE

———— ⟫⟪ ————

This book will help you climb higher, faster in reaching your career goals. It presents ninety concepts to assist and lead you in your climb to success. They are divided into two categories: Management Style and Management Skills. Each concept—guideline, suggestion, tool, ploy, counterploy—covers a specific practical area or situation in management and indicates why, how, and when you should use it.

You will be able to understand and deal better with common problems, issues, and concerns that confront individuals at all levels in all types of organizations. The areas include supervision, leadership, motivation, human relations, planning, evaluation, decision making, budgeting, operating style, organizing, advancing yourself, protecting yourself, and many others. The problems and concerns are real; the suggested approaches are practical and simple, yet concretely stated.

The approaches and solutions, which are quickly and easily read, will be of immediate help and will assist you throughout your career. They deal with many concerns in a way that your professors, colleagues, and mentors rarely do. They provide a common-sense approach to various problems that is based on sound management theory and experience. They capture the essence of the problem and the solution in their one-sentence chapter titles and kernels of wisdom and, thus, allow you to easily remember and apply them. The concepts are practical and strong. They work!

In addition, the book provides a way in which, based on your own experience, you can modify the concepts and add new ones. It therefore becomes a very personal reference and guidebook that can be used time and time again in various situations. Many of the guidelines for improvement and success in one's job and career are applicable in personal relationships and situations and in off-the-job activities, business dealings, and interests. An Appendix at the end of the book highlights the applicability of these concepts and allows you to record and evaluate the results so that in this area, too, the book becomes a personal reference and guidebook.

The need for outstanding management is apparent in every industry and sector of American life. This book can provide the motivation, foundation, and reference for your success now and in the future and for your continued growth and learning.

CONTENTS

II MANAGEMENT SKILLS

INTRODUCTION

Good management is both an art and a science. It is tough, challenging, and exhilarating. The successful practitioner in all types of organizations is concerned with planning, organizing, staffing, deciding, budgeting, innovating, communicating, representing, controlling, and directing. These are aspects of the science of management, although a good deal of art is involved in the practice of the science. The art of management involves empathy, sensitivity, leadership, creativity, a concern for organizational environment, culture, and feelings. The executive plays various roles requiring an effective style and substantive skills. You are a colleague, peer, subordinate, superior, student, teacher, mentor, and role model. In the course of your career, even in the course of your present work month or week, and perhaps daily and hourly, you will in one way or another need to use the skills, insights, and attitudes of one or more types of people. These include planner, dreamer, artist, technician, salesperson, auditor, counselor, preacher, warrior, diplomat, street fighter, and philosopher.

We need to improve our management—in all organizations, in all sectors of the economy—and we have to believe with a passion that we have the ability to meet the challenge. As a nation we have not been particularly successful in dealing with increased international competition. The creativity, quality, price, and durability of our various goods and services have been called into question. As customers, clients, and consumers, in dealing with business, education, government, and nonprofit organizations, we have been exposed to rather frequent instances of incompetence, inefficiency, not caring, sloppiness, shoddiness, insensitivity, and inhumanity. As executives, managers, professionals, and staff members, if we were really honest with ourselves we might see how others would apply some of the same terms to us and our organizations.

Managers and organizations committed to excellence recognize the critical importance of high motivation and sound judgment. Success is more likely to come to those individuals, units, and companies that create and maintain an environment in which there are caring and commitment, risk-taking and a seeking to discover, tough-minded optimism, a zest in being interested and interesting, and confidence in oneself and in others. All of these attributes help colleagues at every level to develop confidence in themselves as well as in other individuals, thereby creating a snowballing effect. As leaders we guide and help, we plan, influence, motivate, and direct. Perhaps most important, we nurture. Fundamental to our multifaceted role is a strong belief in the possibilities and potential in ourselves, in others, and in our organizations.

This book has been written to deal with the various aspects of the art and science of management in a way that will be useful in making you considerably more successful so that you can reach your goals. At the same time, by using the management approaches, techniques, and suggestions contained in the two major sections of the book, Styles and Skills, you can improve the performance of your colleagues and subordinates so that they can better realize their goals. If you and your colleagues are able to improve and strive for excellence, so will your departments or units, thereby uplifting and upgrading your organizations and industries, allowing our society to become more effective and productive. The end result will be greater economic strength, improved goods and services, increased job satisfaction, better organizations, and greater economic and psychological well-being for American society as a whole.

Further, many of the book's concepts can help you in meeting the challenges of everyday life. The approach and content of the book can help you be more successful in: how you relate and interact with spouses and significant others, children and parents, friends, relatives, and all those you come in contact with; the process and results you achieve in buying and selling, negotiating, planning, and making decisions; your ability to handle the stresses and strains, incidents, passages, milestones and life events, the joys and opportunities, victories and defeats, each of us faces. The same drive and commitment called for in understanding and applying these concepts in order to achieve increased success and personal and professional satisfaction in your job and career will be necessary in these other areas. However, the positive results can be very similar and therefore on both the job/career and personal level, your sense of satisfaction, fulfillment and happiness can be greatly enhanced.

It can be done. It takes passion, drive, and commitment, and it all begins with the individual. If you are willing to put forth the passion, drive, and commitment, now and in the future, this book can help you reach success.

I

MANAGEMENT STYLES

1

THE HEART OF THE MATTER

By now, we are all almost tired of hearing the litany of nostrums for America's economic and management problems—lower taxes to create incentives for business and individuals; encourage savings by individuals and capital investments by business; reindustrialize and deregulate American business; emphasize productivity and motivation, quality circles, and quality of life issues; look to high technology, computerization, and robots, and so forth.

But what is often missed in the discussion is the need to emphasize entrepreneurship, risk-taking, zest, and enthusiasm for outstanding management, high standards, and aspirations. We seem to be jogging, holding ourselves in, advancing ploddingly and slowly. We should be sprinting and running full-out to achieve immediate and short-term creativity, innovation, and success. We should also be prepared for running the marathon: looking far ahead; planning and advancing for the long pull; and setting objectives for accomplishment 5, 10, and more years down the road. Too often as managers and organizations we fall prey to being lazy, sloppy, fat, sassy, and tolerant of mediocrity and merely getting by. This, coupled with our concern for the here and now, the good life, hobbies and activities beyond the job, has led to a de-emphasis of the need for excellence in what we do. The value of standards, hard work, praise, and recognition has been debased, and this devaluation has permeated not only companies and organizations but our educational systems as well. We have become too much of a permissive, "laid-back," mediocre-level-of-aspiration society, and this influence affects each individual from kindergarten, through graduate school, through the upper levels of management.

American businesses have been too much concerned with short-term profits and dividends and too little concerned with the future and with their employees' motivation, job satisfaction, and ideas. We overemphasize numbers, computers, and quantitative analysis. Too many executives and recent graduates with MBA degrees have either lost or never acquired the entrepreneurial passion for making tough decisions and taking significant risks. Wrapped up in numbers, financial analysis, and management information system reports, they have become too remote from the heart of the enterprise they manage and from the concerns of customers and employees, the markets, the technology of today and tomorrow.

Low productivity is discussed ad nauseam but instead of blaming only workers, high taxes, small incentives, governmental regulations, and unions, we should also blame poor management planning, commitment, decision making, and foresight.

We should recognize in ourselves and American society that we accept or just shrug when we note a pervasive lack of pride in craftsmanship and quality of work or service. Our society appears to turn out, more so than ever before, people who expect praise, promotion, a bonus, a gratuity, a large increase for inadequate or merely satisfactory performance. That ought not to be enough for ourselves, our organizations, our staffs, our corporate and national leaders, our nation as a whole.

Good management can be exciting and stimulating. Managerial tasks should be approached with vigor and enthusiasm. We tend as professional, successful managers to be calm, cool, and collected decision makers and rational managers. While this is valuable, we need more fire, more passion and concern as we strive to achieve, to do better, to be better.

From kindergarten through graduate or professional school, from the individual's first day in an organization to his or her last, we should set and require high standards. We should assist the individual, provide the opportunities, challenges, resources, training, incentives, and rewards, but for him or her and ourselves the goal should be consistent, outstanding, superb performance. We should emphasize talent, enthusiasm, hard work, and striving for true distinction. Whatever an individual's job or position, we must develop the organization structure, environment, and concern that encourage, demand, and reward full effort to the best of the individual's ability. We must seek to improve each individual's ability and satisfaction. In addition to technical knowledge, technology, and techniques, the successful executive needs to have the power and influence of interpersonal skills, personality, drive, empathy, and zest.

As managers and executives, we are rightfully concerned about success and profits for the organization, short and long term, and maximizing income for ourselves, our subordinates, and all who help the organization achieve its objectives.

However, we live by more than bread and conspicuous consumption. Increasingly, an important aspect of motivation, satisfaction, and productivity is psychic income: recognition, job stimulation and challenge, learning, growth, maximum utilization of one's abilities, high standards, a sense of mission, accomplishment, and team effort. Such income can come about for ourselves and for others through an organization's concern, climate, culture, and an emphasis on human needs and aspirations.

The challenge for executives at all levels is to reach beyond their grasp; to strive for true excellence; and to set ambitious and challenging goals for themselves, their units, and their organizations. Complacency and acceptance of what currently exists must give way to a sense of challenge and a healthy dissatisfaction with the status quo. The acceptance and practice of the attitude and philosophy suggested in this book lead to striving for higher organizational and personal goals and standards and to developing, leading, motivating, and working with others to reach for the top. The result can be exhilaration and joy in meeting great expectations.

The goals set forth are indeed tough, requiring the best that we can offer as individuals and as organizations. We will need a renewed passion to succeed, to make our particular organizations better, more productive, challenging, and satisfying. We need to emphasize an ethic based on performance, results, and self-actualization that not only requires great effort, effectiveness, and efficiency but involves learning, growth, pride, progress, purpose, people, and a concern for quality craftsmanship, and high standards of production and service. Our credo might well be taken from Theodore Roosevelt's statement, "To the Man in the Arena":

It is not the critic that counts nor the man who points out how the strong man stumbled or where the doer of deeds could have done them better.

The credit belongs to the man who is actually in the arena; whose face is marred by dust and sweat and blood; who strives valiantly . . . ; who knows the great enthusiasms, the great devotions, and spends himself in a worthy cause; who, at his best, knows the triumph of high achievement; and who, at his worst, if he fails, at least fails while daring greatly, so that his place shall never be with those cold and timid souls who know neither victory nor defeat.*

*The Works of Theodore Roosevelt, Herman Hagedorn (ed.), National edition, 20 vols. New York: Scribner, 1926. Vol. 13, p. 510.

2

GOOD ENOUGH ISN'T GOOD ENOUGH

By and large, most organizations and the people in them have become "good enough" advocates. Our pride and insistence on excellence, on quality, on doing considerably more than what would suffice have been eroded. We are satisfied with "good enough."

We can rationalize this trying to do enough but not much more by saying people won't pay for, recognize, or appreciate extra effort; we don't have the time or resources to go the extra mile; workers aren't as motivated as they used to be and thus won't work harder or better, or will want extra pay for everything. But whether it is in elementary school or college, on the assembly line or in the executive suite, because of habit, pressures, costs, or fear of upsetting people, we demand too little of ourselves and others.

We need to become more of a nation of complainers or, better said, a nation that won't accept inadequate quality or performance for the payment of an adequate price. We have the right to expect satisfactory performance and to reward with our patronage and praise those who have risen above satisfactory performance and mediocrity to excellent performance and superiority.

As managers, we will have to set higher standards and tougher goals; we will need to see that our subordinates, and indeed ourselves, are properly trained, motivated, and rewarded in regard to doing more than just getting by. It is true that we will have to balance costs and benefits and realize that many will not recognize that something beyond the ordinary is being done or that a concern for being better may carry a price others won't pay. However, if we can seek to raise our standards significantly, steadily, and continuously, we can produce better products and develop a better workforce, better managers, and ultimately a better organization. The sense that Company X is better will gradually become known to customers, clients, and those whose support determines the company's success. I would argue that practically all organizations can be price competitive yet at the same time maintain standards of service, concern, civility, and interest in the customer that set the company apart from others. From a de facto "good enough is good enough" philosophy, there can be a turn toward, "we're good and striving to get better." This will require considerable attention to detail, to quality control, to nit-picking, to paying more and doing more, to more training and different reward systems, to more careful evaluation of performance. It will require us to drop "it's good enough" or "it's OK" from our lexicon and to stress "that's good, that's excellent." Whether it is how we answer the telephone, the content or typing of a letter, the quality of product or service, the timeliness of delivery, the keeping of promises, or following up, all aspects of endeavor will have to be covered. This dedication to going beyond the usual will have to extend not only to front-line operations, but to the back rooms as well. Throughout the organization, from the lowest to the highest paid, there should be pride that we're different, we're better, we care. We care for our customers and clients, we care for our employees as people, we care about our organization.

Those organizations that can effectively establish themselves as anti-good-enoughers will be able to create a climate and environment that leads to further successes within the organization and in meeting the competition. In effect, a mystique can be crated that strengthens the individual within the organization and the organization itself. If we want to improve ourselves and our companies, to create greater satisfaction and pride for workers and managers, it's time we buried the "good enough" philosophy—it just isn't good enough any longer.

3

TRYING HARD ISN'T ENOUGH—
RESULTS ARE WHAT COUNT

————————— ✦✕✦ —————————

Management ought not to be like some elementary-school classes where as long as you attend all the time, don't disrupt the class, and make a good effort, you get a passing grade. It is important to care, to give all that one has, all the time. Loyalty and dedication are certainly admirable traits. Working long and hard is to be praised and rewarded. But after all is said and done, the issue is: No matter how hard you've worked or tried, what are the results?

Too often we tend to forgive or forget poor results or failure because of the diligence one has demonstrated and the time, effort, sweat, and ego invested in the failed project. We let our admiration for the effort, and recognition of the difficulty of the task, cloud or overwhelm our assessment of the poor results obtained and the reasons for failure. Certainly, we should recognize impossible-to-achieve assignments or extremely tough challenges when failure is almost certain or highly likely. In those cases, effort indeed should be praised and poor results evaluated, but not held against the individual or team. In fact, coming close to achieving the goal may be the most one could hope for, given uncontrollable situations or factors that may have arisen.

My point is that for most circumstances, problems, and projects, supervisors and evaluators must care about outcomes. There should be an assessment as to why there was success or failure of the actual versus the planned. There should be a strategy for improving future performance. For example, our planning assumptions or conclusions might have been inaccurate or too optimistic. On the other hand, performance and results for one reason or another, may not have reached the level they should have. Obviously, we want to learn from our failures (and successes) in order to improve our planning, project team selection, training of individuals and project teams, implementation techniques, and so forth.

The organization should discourage cutting corners and use of shoddy or dirty practices in order to achieve internal or external success. We indeed want to bring about in the organization a sense of constantly trying hard, with integrity, to achieve goals. But what should receive even more attention and praise than how hard one tried and how good a race for success one ran, is whether one crossed the finish line and achieved the goal.

4

THE COMPLACENCY TRAP

If things are going well in your unit and company, it's easy to become complacent and satisfied. After all, your increases and bonuses have been above average, good, or excellent, and your track record merits acclaim. From a company or unit view, sales, profits, share of market, return on investment, and so on, have been increasing either in line with projections or even better. These factors should lead an individual to feel satisfied with past and present performance and to look forward with confidence to the future.

At the same time that one views accomplishments with pride, there is a need to strike a balance so that satisfaction doesn't become complacency, and striving for continued and increased achievement doesn't turn into resting on one's laurels. It is all too easy to slow down and coast for a while or a long time once ambitious goals have been met and one's hunger for recognition, profits, and so on, have been fulfilled.

You should be proud of past and present successes and you deserve, whether as an individual or a company, to take a breather in scaling high mountains of challenges and competition. But you must be careful not to fall prey to taking too long a rest, to basking in past glories, and to hesitating to enter the fray again.

Though seeking to be basically satisfied with yourself, your unit, and your company, it pays to resist a strong temptation to let things be since just about everything appears to be going pretty well. One needs a healthy dissatisfaction with the status quo and with a future that appears to be only a continuation of the present. By "healthy," I don't mean stirring things or yourself up just for the sake of being energetic or exercising managerial authority. One needs to balance satisfaction with fine accomplishments and striving to do better. Of course, if your own or your company's performance hasn't been good, it's easy to be dissatisfied and to devote thought and resources to improvements. The more difficult task is to question performance and seek even greater accomplishments when things are going rather well.

In essence, a healthy dissatisfaction would call for setting ambitious, but not outlandish, goals and objectives, and providing the climate, resources, and incentives for people to have the desire, ability, and means to meet these high expectations. It requires you to look, from time to time, at everything you do and how you do it to see whether you can make major or even minor improvements. Your goals, objectives, policies, procedures, and practices should be looked at from a questioning point of view. Am I on the right track? What would happen if I looked for alternatives in all areas—what would be the positive and negative consequences? Assume I must change everything I'm doing—how would I do it? If I were starting from scratch or forming a competitive company, what would I do the same, somewhat different, totally different? Whom would I want to take with me if I became president of my major competitor and whom would I not consider at all? Why? If my superior or an expert outside-consulting firm were conducting a detailed review of my area and my personal performance, what things would I be most proud or least proud of, what would I hope they wouldn't discover?

These questions and answers would provide clues as to changes you might want to make in your present position. They invite you to evaluate where you have been and where you are going, to seek greater challenges and opportunities, to provide a spark for yourself and others to go on to greater achievements.

Always questioning, never being satisfied, can result in an un-healthy dissatisfaction with today and tomorrow. Thus, one must maintain that fine balance of being appreciative and proud of past and present accomplishments while retaining one's desire to do even better now and in the future. You must seek to find that balance to motivate yourself and others to do better without ending up feeling harassed and discontented. In short, one needs, assuming at least good past and present performance, to be striving toward being better without being compulsively driven.

5

GET HOT . . . SOMETIMES

One of the major problems of American management is that we have become so scientific-minded in terms of management that we have forgotten that good management is as much an art as it is a science. We analyze, use quantitative analysis techniques, run computer simulations, apply models. We strive to do all the things they teach in regard to good planning, analysis, problem solving, and decision making. All of this is important, but we should be careful that we don't become so analytically cool that we forgo the opportunities to operate emotionally hot.

What we need is a balance between greatly hedging our bets, assessing risk so carefully that we attempt as little as possible at somewhat diminished returns versus acting impulsively and emotionally, thereby greatly increasing the chances for disaster—and success. You can even try to meld the two approaches, very careful analysis and minimization of risk with willingness to take bigger chances, by including as two of the factors in your study of a situation your gut or emotional reaction and your ability and willingness to take big risks in return for significantly greater rewards.

Another aspect of this issue is that you have to decide how aggressive you should be in choosing a course of action or implementing your decision now. Do you really go after what you want in the most direct or toughest fashion or do you go more slowly, perhaps somewhat indirectly and softly, thereby occasionally losing some of the results expected, but not upsetting people or situations as much? In both aspects, the basic issue is how much of your energy and emotion, resources, and reputation you are willing to expend to accomplish your goal. How much of a risk-taker are you? There is no "correct" answer to the question of "how much." It will depend on your own style and personality, the situation, the organization, and the general environment. Some people are gamblers, others are not. Some place $2 bets on the favorite to show and thus may earn $2.60. They are pleased not so much with the 60 cents they won, but that they didn't lose $2. Others will place $100 on the long shot to win, hoping that they'll earn $3,000.

In my experience, it seems that people increasingly choose to protect themselves against big or even slight loss and are satisfied by relatively small gains. Of course, there will always be individuals who will gamble everything on coming up with the big deal and payoff, but there seem to be fewer of these people than in the past. We seem to shy away from very tough goals for our organizations, units, and even for ourselves. I would argue that it is important to be prudent and careful, but at least some of the time let your visions and striving be great. You may laugh at yourself or kick yourself later for having put so much into what didn't pay off very much or in hindsight seems to be rather unimportant. Even if you fail, there's great value and learning gained from tackling the seemingly impossible. Even if the goal isn't that large, it pays to condition yourself to run as fast as you can and try as hard as you can for those things that seem important to you.

But whether on the job or off, if something is important to you, it's worth it, from time to time, to let it all hang out, to go for it with all you've got. You don't want to waste your all-out attempts because there's a limit to what your reputation, results, energy, and emotion can stand. But, neither do you want to hold it all in waiting for the right moment or the prize worth seeking because if you try to run that all-out race very rarely you may find you can't get started, don't have the stamina, can't keep pace with other runners, or have lost your kick at the end. So, no matter how small a risk-taker you are, once in a while, let it all hang out—go for it!

6

TREAT EVERYONE ALIKE, BUT NOT THE SAME

Early in my career, I had a veteran supervisor who was respected and successful. He once described his management philosophy to me with great pride as being "treat everyone the same." It took quite a while before I realized that he was wrong.

I suggest that you should treat everyone alike in terms of being fair and decent, and applying organizational rules, practices, evaluation systems in a fair, impartial, and nondiscriminatory way. All in your unit and the organization should come to expect a general consistency in your approach and style when dealing with issues and people.

However, this does not mean that you treat everyone the same. Each of us is different. What motivates me may not motivate you. A supervisor may need to give some people pats on the back and others kicks in the rear. Although a supervisor should be fair to all, he or she may deliberately be tougher on some than others in order to bring forth effort or develop potential. Some employees are self-starters, others have to have things outlined in considerable detail. Some want or need constantly to check things out with the supervisor, others function best (and it works out best for the organization) if the supervisor just sets broad guidelines and sees them very rarely. Goading, praising, cracking the whip, holding hands, public compliments, private reprimands—all of these and other approaches may need to be applied to the various members in the unit. The sophisticated supervisor assesses the personality and skills of each subordinate and, while keeping to a generally consistent style (employees don't work well with erratic supervisors), applies different techniques to different individuals. In fact, depending on the assignment and the stage in the individual's career or previous performance, the supervisor may employ different approaches at different times in supervising the same person.

In treating people in different ways depending on an assessment of what works best with the particular individual, it's important to be careful that it does not seem like outright favoritism or hostility. The supervisor should, therefore, accomplish his or her goals through applying approaches in private in a one-on-one situation (although at times, public approaches will be necessary).

The selective approach geared to particular people and situations requires an investment of more thought, time, and effort by supervisors, but the results achieved far outweigh the costs.

7

BE KIND TO THOSE COMING IN AND GOING OUT

Just as you often remember your first "true" love, it is likely that you will remember the first person on the job who was kind to you or befriended you. The newcomer to an organization or to a new position or unit within the organization, no matter how high the position or confident the person, has certain concerns and trepidations.

The person within the organization, whether superior, colleague, or subordinate, who reaches out even a bit beyond the call of duty, generally receives the immediate and lasting gratitude of the new person. Ways of reaching out range from calling the person before he or she reports to the new job (if you have found out a new employee is coming) to indicate that you look forward to working with him or her and offer your help in any way (advice as to where to live, banks, real estate agents, schools, and so forth, if relocation is involved); to inviting the individual for coffee or lunch the first day on the job and introducing him or her to others; to familiarizing the person with procedures, resources, facilities, and so on. You will, if successful, have begun a good and perhaps important working relationship that may bring you a new personal friend, a friendly colleague at work, or someone who can help you in accomplishing your goals.

Unfortunately, while most of us can focus on the problems of the newcomer and see that it may be in our personal interest to be kind, we often don't go out of our way for the person who is retiring or leaving voluntarily or involuntarily. Those who are going, though the reasons and circumstances may vary greatly, also face trepidations and concerns, probably more serious and difficult ones than the newcomer. Thus, depending upon the situation, an offer of assistance or support; a recognition of the person's contributions to the organization; a suggestion about contacts in or for new positions together with an offer to follow up on them or to serve as a reference; discussion of retirement plans; follow-up calls or notes after the person has left—all will mark you as a kind and concerned individual. And you never know when the reputation you have earned, or action by the person for whom you went a bit out of your way, could be of help to you in your current or future job. In essence, the point is simple: Treat those in the revolving door of organizational life in a manner such as you would hope to be treated in a similar situation, but would not really expect to happen.

8

RESIST REVENGE

———————— ⟫✦⟪ ————————

There will be times (many, I hope) when you gain the upper hand in a negotiation, deal, situation, or crisis. You have won the contest, race, or "war." You feel entitled to enjoy the exhilaration of winning, of victory, of having fought a tough battle and having emerged triumphant. It is natural for you to want to reap the fruits of your victory, or to follow, in the old political sense, "to the victor belongs the spoils." After all, there should be ample reward for having pulled off a big deal, or a successful action in the face of competition and tough odds.

Certainly, you are entitled to whatever monetary and nonmonetary rewards the situation warrants. But you should be wary of a normal tendency, particularly if the battle has been tough, hard, and dirty, to really vanquish your foe—a competitor, union head, fellow executive who has opposed you, or someone of that sort. There is often a personal desire, or a desire by those who have worked with you, to make it really tough for your opponent, to get even, to make the person bleed a bit (if not a lot), to rub the loser's nose in it. This feeling, which at times can become an overwhelming, almost unconquerable drive, should be acknowledged, understood, and combated.

It is fair to admit to yourself that aside from perhaps being a bit bloodthirsty (something you should attempt to conquer or at least modify), there may be good reason for you to want to extract all you can, not only in terms of the specifics of the situation, but also in terms of humbling your foe. He or she may have engaged in various dirty tricks, lacked integrity, or impugned your honor. He or she may be the type of person who, if the tables had been turned, would certainly have kicked you very hard while you were down. You might have matched dirty tactic for dirty tactic during the contest. Alternatively, you might have taken the high road to the other's low road. In either case, there may be a pent-up desire, now with victory assured, to get even and to punish in order to teach a lesson and/or to receive satisfaction. In effect, do unto others, doubly, what they did or would do unto you.

As satisfying as revenge might be, I suggest that a certain degree of understanding of the impact of defeat on the other person or company, of empathy with him, or her, or it, of allowing your opponent to retain a sense of self and a sense of worthiness and honor is important for your foe, but also for you. In essence, some degree of gallantry in victory, even though you may deplore the tactics your opponent employed, can be a very effective and human thing for you to display. Your ability to cease from inflicting additional harm or embarrassment when your foe knows you could have, demonstrates strength, reason, a sense of professionalism, personal style, and integrity that your foe and/or at least your colleagues and others will respect and admire. In many cases, it creates a sense of obligation on the part of those who have lost to you, but not been embarrassed by you, to remember the way you acted in victory. This can be of great help to your relationship with them or those they know and to your general reputation in any future dealings you may have. People remember those who acted with restraint, with a sense of dignity and professionalism, and in most cases they feel obligated to repay the debt in one way or another.

If you are still unable to fight off a desire really to rub the person's nose in it, remember you may lose the next battle to this opponent or to those who know how you acted when you won. And they, like you, may not be able to control the desire, particularly in light of how you acted.

9

SUCCESS HAS MANY FATHERS;
FAILURE IS AN ORPHAN

When there is a celebration of the success of a venture or project, you have to look for a very large room to acknowledge those who contributed greatly or to some slight degree as well as those who think or claim they did. Every one wants a piece of the glory no matter how small the actual contribution. We all want to be part of the winning team and as months or years go by, just as the college or professional athlete tends to exaggerate past successes and contributions to the team, so do we tend to exaggerate our management contributions.

But when there is a failure, one needs only a very small room to invite those to commemorate the defeat or to evaluate the lessons learned because many will shun the invitation (unless they are forced) or claim that they had little or no part in the decision or action. Recriminations; alibis; the casting of stones; and the blaming of others, bad luck, or outside forces are some of the things likely to be heard at such meetings. And the reasons for failure suggested by those involved will usually include poor planning; lack of sufficient authority or resources; poor or unclear communications; weak organization and staffing; lack of thorough, accurate, and timely information; and failure to decide or act decisively.

It is important to learn lessons from our successes so that the strategies, tactics, and approaches can be utilized, modified as necessary, in other situations. It is probably more important to learn from our failures because we will probably dissect them much more thoroughly and, thus, learn valuable, though bitter, lessons.

In order to improve your chances to be in the large room celebrating rather than in the small room sweating, it is important to have some understanding of how to solve problems and make decisions and also how to involve others appropriately so that they share responsibility with you. Of course, if you're the top person, some or much of the glory will go to you and most or all of the blame.

You will want to involve others in any major undertaking to enable you to gather the brainpower necessary to meet the problems, to utilize the resources of their units, and to ensure that you are covering all the appropriate areas in dealing with the situation. You want and need others to "buy in" to the problem and solution, and to work with you to bring about favorable results. Depending on the complexity of the matter, you may have to worry about organizing project teams or other approaches. But the point is, you need the involvement of others, not only to solve the problem, but also to demonstrate your concern for the appropriate depth and breadth of involvement. This also protects you against others saying, "If only I had been consulted, I would have . . . " You can take your chances and try to be the hero who singlehandedly tackled the issue rather than sharing the responsibility and glory. The odds are rather good, however, that if you do that, you will indeed be the lonely orphan when failure occurs, as is likely if others aren't involved.

10

EARNING "A'S" AS A SUPERVISOR— AVAILABILITY, ACCESSIBILITY, AFFABILITY, ABILITY

After all is said and done about a supervisor's technical, managerial, and interpersonal skills, everything may boil down to four "A's." In descending order of importance, these are Availability, Accessibility, Affability, and Ability.

Availability. A subordinate needs and likes to know that his or her supervisor is available for consultation and guidance; providing assignments, opportunities, approval for a course of action; providing information, support, timely evaluation of one's work effort. All too often, the supervisor is not physically present often enough or is too busy to deal in depth or at all with the concerns and issues facing the subordinate. Thus, whether it's a timely response to a request for a meeting or to a note, memo, or completed project, the subordinate wants to feel that he or she can see or get a response from the boss and get enough uninterrupted time and attention.

Accessibility. The successful supervisor is able to demonstrate that he or she has access to higher authority, to various resources, to information. By being able to get support and authority when necessary, he or she is able to provide needed authority, resources, and information to subordinates so that they can be more effective in accomplishing their missions. Your subordinates' knowing that their boss has respect and influence in the organization can be very helpful in building morale and confidence in the unit and, thus, improves their performance, which earns the boss and the subordinates even further respect and influence in the organization.

Affability. The boss need not be a stand-up comic, life of the party, or glad hander. However, the successful supervisor has a certain degree of affability—a liking for people and an interest in them, an appreciation for humor, a lack of pomposity and of taking oneself too seriously. He or she is a person you feel comfortable talking with about work issues as well as general issues and is a good and interested listener.

Ability. Finally, there is sheer ability. The effective supervisor knows the objectives to be accomplished and how and what to do. He or she has the technical knowledge (though some, many, or all of his or her subordinates may know more) and the managerial and interpersonal skills to get the job done successfully. He or she is a leader and motivator, skilled at planning, implementing, directing, controlling, organizing, budgeting, deciding, innovating, communicating, staffing, and representing the unit.

One cannot be truly successful without considerable strength in all four A's. Normally, one always selects ability as the first criterion for success, but in the long run great ability without significant strength in regard to availability, accessibility, and affability will lead to mediocre performance or worse.

11

Seeing and Believing

"Assume that things are as they appear to be" is not bad advice. In fact, one can call that the Face Value Theory of Management. What you see is really what is; there are no hidden agendas, the piece of ice floating on the water is not the tip of an iceberg, but merely a piece of ice. Adherence to this view helps you reach conclusions faster because you don't search for other explanations or complex interpretations or hidden meanings. You also avoid feeling paranoid.

Equally valid is the idea that important things are not as simple as they may appear and that you must probe and look for different meanings and motives. Adherence to this view prolongs decision making, but may produce better decisions and actions.

Generally, whether one is likely to be more successful using the face value theory, or the view that there's more to things than meets the eye, will depend on the person's skills, experience, and personality, knowledge of and trust in colleagues and subordinates, and the importance of the matter. I would urge that you assume that there may be more to a matter than meets the eye in the following circumstances: Big bucks are involved in the decision; it sets a precedent; it will have an important impact on you, your unit, other units, or the company, now and/or in the future. If time permits (sometimes it will not, but you should try to schedule things so that there is a sufficient period for review), you should spend time asking questions about the assumptions, data, analytical techniques, and results of consultations held with others who have knowledge and/or will be affected by the decision.

Although I generally suggest that, on important matters, you avoid the face value theory, I also suggest that often there is less to things than your emotions say. Often those in middle and upper management get overly suspicious of people, data, and conditions, and overly fearful of what will go wrong. Their emotions take hold and they end up saying, "the solution or suggestion is too good (bad); something must have been overlooked, or someone is kidding me or trying to mislead me."

The successful manager learns basically as a result of his or her experience with issues, the organization, and the providers of information and suggestions (who occasionally make mistakes) how to decide on each matter, whether to assume that there's less to things than meets the eye or more than the emotions say.

12

CONTROLLED RAGE CAN BE USEFUL

In this era of concern about "body language," we all know or think we know what people are telling us with their body movements or nonmovements, seated and standing positions, facial expressions, eye movements, and other types of nonverbal communication. It pays to look into these matters because they may be helpful to you in dealing with others in terms of getting signals and either intentionally giving or not giving them. However, one must be careful not to assume that body-language signals are always accurately portraying the person's view.

It is important, in many cases, to try to keep a poker face in terms of expressing your reactions to the issues presented to you. This allows you to appear calm and unruffled, no matter what the problem, and it does not signal what you might be thinking of doing. At times, it will be difficult to maintain that unperturbed expression. The poker face can also be an effective tool in driving your opponent in a negotiation or dispute to distraction since he or she may be seeking to "read" your expressions in terms of what he or she might be able to achieve.

At the same time that I indicate the value, in general, of a poker face it should be noted that sometimes you want to indicate your reactions. This can be by your expression—no longer a poker face—your body language, your words, your animation, and so on. Whatever you show, as far as possible, should be by design rather than accidental. Sometimes this will be a natural and normal action or expression that you don't attempt to harness or control and it thus just comes out. Other times, you will carefully plan when and how to react and your seemingly spontaneous reaction may indeed be premeditated.

Your expressiveness can range from absolute dullness, to poker face, to controlled rage. By controlled rage, I mean very strong opposition or anger to the subject matter and tone of the conversation, to the memo or report, perhaps even including anger toward personalities. I emphasize controlled in two aspects. First, that no matter what the provocation, you steel yourself to keep your rage within the bounds of rational behavior. Second, that you may want to "ham" it up a bit and express greater anger than you really feel in order to make a point or elicit some reaction or changed behavior on the part of those at whom your anger is directed.

The point is that your expressions, tone, and style of dealing with problems are important factors in your overall managerial effectiveness. You should carefully evaluate how you usually react to annoyances, day-to-day problems, and crises to determine whether your style of reactions helps or hinders the accomplishment of your objectives, your leadership, and your motivation of staff. It may be that you will have to force yourself to be more calm, or alternatively, to show more controlled rage. You will also learn in time that your style, either naturally or by design, will vary depending on the situation and the individuals involved. In essence, the poker face is a good general approach, but you will need to modify it as part of your arsenal of techniques in becoming a more successful manager.

13

PROTECT YOUR REAR, SHARPEN YOUR ELBOWS

One hopes and expects that in the work situation professionalism, integrity, candor, and civility will prevail. There are times, however, when the politics and in-fighting, backbiting, gamesmanship, and one-upsmanship can become rather severe. The person who chooses not to defend or protect himself or herself, does so inadequately, or does not have a sensitivity and early warning system concerning possible attacks, will find himself or herself at a disadvantage, severely injured, or looking for a new job. One need not be cynical about human nature, paranoid, or distrustful, in order to be concerned about not getting slashed up, for whatever reason, by others.

As a general safety measure and risk-reduction approach, it is wise to pay some attention to protecting your rear. This doesn't mean that you have to spend so much time and effort on self-protection that you are unable to accomplish your objectives or be perceived as never taking a forthright stand. It does mean that you show a prudent concern for not leaving yourself too exposed in case someone wants to take a shot at you, so that at least the shot won't be fatal.

Sometimes you will have to risk things and leave yourself unprotected because of the demands of the particular situation. The decision you will have to make is, What are the risks to me, my unit, and my company if I let it all hang out?

There are several ways you can provide minimal protection of your rear. These are general guidelines that should be adapted to particular situations, personalities, conditions, and times in an organization's life.

1. Gather as much reliable and timely information as possible as a basis for your decision or action.

2. Be careful whom you tell what, in writing and orally, and be sensitive to who might hear or see what you are communicating. Make sure you can trust the person in whom you confide.

3. Consult as broadly and as deeply as possible. Indicate your concerns, if there are any, in regard to target date, resources, responsibility, and authority made available to you.

4. Document your assumptions and the bases on which decisions were made, including the materials used in the analysis and the providers of the raw or analyzed data. You certainly have the responsibility to ask the right questions and to verify and evaluate the analysis, where possible, but if someone made an error in the calculations or analysis, at least that should be known.

5. Plan the aspects of the assignment thoroughly, document your plans, evaluate them at various times, modify and update as necessary, have others review them.

6. Try to get "partners" where possible—that is, involve others and where appropriate have them join with you in making the proposal or decision or at least indicate their support—in this way you share the glory to some extent, but you also share the responsibility and demonstrate that it wasn't a one-person show. Indicate that you are involved in a team or consensus effort.

7. Get appropriate people to approve and/or commit, in writing, to various aspects of planning and implementation.

8. Keep your supervisor thoroughly and regularly briefed, preferably in writing, as to plans, analysis, decision points, implementation, and evaluation. Where appropriate, solicit his or her advice, approval, and decision.

9. Conduct an evaluation after the fact and be objective in pointing out accomplishments and failures.

10. Assuming moderate to complete success, share the glory, orally and in writing.

There are times when you will have to be combative. While other sections of this book deal with the matter in different ways, here I suggest ways to sharpen your elbows so that you hold your own or prevail in the shoving and jockeying for position, slight advantage, and one-upsmanship that often take place.

1. If you don't trust a person's ability to keep things in confidence, you may want to plant a story with him or her or use the person to float a trial balloon.

2. When necessary, keep your views sufficiently vague and ambiguous so that if you have to, you can claim that you were misinterpreted.

3. Leak information or transmit rumors, if it is in your interest to do so. Remember, you run a real risk of getting fired if you get caught so it better be worth your while (it rarely is).

4. Go around your boss to his or her colleague, rival, or boss. This is dangerous and should only be done as a last resort. If your boss finds out and has sufficient power, be prepared to be sending out your resumé or, better yet, be prepared to start your own business because when others call for a reference check, your boss will attempt to kill you. If he or she doesn't have sufficient power to fire you, you may still find life very uncomfortable.

5. Wait to speak up, sense the drift of the meeting, rehearse what you're going to say, and then present your views, indicating how others have contributed to them. At the same time, show why the discussion clearly reflects your view—the consensus view—which is correct, while your rival's is incorrect.

6. Check your rival's data, analysis, sources, in a quiet fashion. Then point out in a manner and form that strengthens your position and weakens his or hers, the gaps, errors, incomplete work, faulty interpretation of data, and so forth.

7. When necessary, indicate by body language, facial expressions, and choice of words your disagreement with others' views.

Your words can be carefully chosen so they do not seem to be a totally unfair blast, but remain in others' minds and, thus, influence their decision and their regard for you and the individual you oppose. You should regard the following as darts or weapons that should be used sparingly, but in an effective fashion. Too frequent or inappropriate use weakens their impact and hurts you. Sentences that sting:

- "I know that Joe has done a great deal of work on this under a very tight deadline, and I don't know whether he had sufficient time, given the deadline and his other responsibilities, but I believe he overlooked . . . "

- "To be brief and candid about my reaction, I regret that I have to say there's less to this than meets the eye."

- "I believe the situation demands a unique, creative approach; instead we have a solid, thorough, ordinary, humdrum approach."

- "It appears that the best thinking has gone into a very attractive and creative presentation and packaging, but the product is, at the most, barely adequate."

- "She's more interested in the perks and protecting her own turf than what's good for the organization."

- "I don't know why, but you don't appear to be willing to tackle the tough issues."

- "I think he's a good guy and for the first few months I thought he was a great guy, but frankly, I think he's wearing thin."

- "That proposal or plan is all style and no substance."

- "That sounds good, but, frankly, I think you didn't get below the surface and into the practical problems."

- "It seems to me that he is a good thinker and nice guy, but he shies away from getting his hands dirty and rolling up his sleeves."

- "She's got a great staff; without them, she's lost."

- "Joe, I know these are the opinions of your staff, but what are your views?"

- "I hate to say this, but I have reluctantly concluded that she is a first-rate second rater (or this is a very good second-rate effort)."

8. Maneuver to be appointed to the powerful committees and task forces, to be involved in those situations that give you access to and recognition by those in power or with access to power. In this way, you can advance your views and yourself.

9. Establish yourself as a leader in some outside professional, civic, or community group to indicate your breadth and commitment as a person and leader. This will provide prestige as well as access.

10. Through writing, speaking, and serving on committees, attempt to establish yourself as a recognized, respected, and sought-after authority. This will enhance your position in the company and might even get you job offers!

While you should be careful not to overdo protecting your rear and sharpening the elbows, it doesn't hurt to be prepared.

14

WHEN IN COMBAT: LOGIC, TOUGHNESS, AND MERCY

There will be times in your position and career that you will be in various stages of combat with those inside the organization, such as other units and colleagues, superiors, subordinates, union negotiators, and such. You will always face battles with those outside the organization—competitors, government officials, various types of organizations, and the media, for instance. It may be the management equivalent of a brush fire or short skirmish, a battle rather than war, a limited war, a conventional major war, or an all-out "nuclear" war. Hopefully, there will be relatively few battles and wars of various types, but there will certainly be some. It is, therefore, helpful for you to be prepared for combat even though you may do all you can to avoid such incidents and to limit the seriousness of the situation.

As a matter of policy and practice, you will have to decide whether you will engage in first strikes, preventive strikes, or surprise attacks; or respond only after being attacked, fight defensively only, counterattack to drive the enemy off and then attack your foe's soil. You will have to decide with what force you will attack or counterattack and whether your basic strategy is to bring about the cessation of hostilities, and prevent defeat or harm to yourself, versus achieving partial or total victory. Will you ever accept unconditional surrender, or if necessary, will you be willing to accept partial defeat? In regard to your opponent, will you allow a stalemate, return to the status quo ante, a partial defeat for the "enemy," or insist on unconditional surrender? The answers to those questions may very well depend on the specific situation and its importance, how combat began and how it was fought, the strength, personality, and strategy of your opponent, and your personality, strength, and strategy.

What is important at the outset of consideration of this matter is the need to control your emotions as much as possible in planning and implementing your strategy and tactics.

The stakes may be high indeed: the independence of the company or unit, the resources available to you, the power, responsibilities, and authority of your position, your unit's reputation, your reputation, your future in the company, your job, your career. But if you lose your cool, you are very likely to lose the battle and the war. Of course, with the adrenaline flowing, bravery and charisma can be of vital importance, but you also need clear thinking.

The combat may involve, at one extreme, mergers, acquisitions, unfriendly takeovers, potential bankruptcy, or crippling strikes, or it may involve differences in regard to policies, procedures, evaluations, compensation, organization, controls, resource allocation, staffing, advertising, production, and other areas.

There may be times when you decide to launch a first strike because you want to beat your opponent to the punch since you believe your foe is about to attack you momentarily. On the other hand, you may want to attack because you know that pretty soon the enemy will attack. Or, you may want to take advantage of a time when you have strength and the enemy is weak to indicate to your opponent (and perhaps others) your power or strength or even "irrationality" in order to warn, hurt, disarm, or totally defeat your foe.

You have to be very careful about first strikes because, in fact, you may not have the correct information about your opponent and striking first may result in your defeat and/or the loss of your reputation instead of partial or total victory and the creation or enhancement of a reputation of being smart and tough. The question will always be: Is the situation sufficiently important and the chances of success sufficiently great for you to attack first?

Assuming the attack was not an all-out attack but relatively minor, there may be instances when you are on the defensive and might have to logically decide whether it is worth it to fight at all. Though it is very difficult to decide not to fight because your ego and emotions are quickly put to the test (particularly if it appears to you to be an unprovoked attack), it may be in your best interests to let the attack pass without reacting and to inform your opponent that you believe this was an inadvertent error on your opponent's part which he or she should correct immediately. Or you can indicate what you will do unless your foe ceases and withdraws. Or, you can ask for cessation of hostilities and withdrawal and/or discussion of the issue(s), perhaps with a third party present. Finally, you can decide to let your enemy have his or her small victory, concede the issue, and try to limit the battle. This is particularly difficult because you and others may regard this as appeasement. However, if you are unprepared, it may be in your best interest to lose a small battle in order not to risk total defeat and thus gain time to gear up for bigger ones or an all-out war.

Once you are in a battle, you should be clear as to what your goals are and what you think your opponent's goals are. Does your enemy just want to hurt your reputation, force you to leave, desire to gain something for himself or herself or for his or her unit, or is it merely an honest difference of opinion with your foe being very forceful in attacking your views and advocating his or hers? Once you decide the importance of the issues and the risks of loss and various kinds of combat, you can then determine what type of response is in your best interests. If you decide to fight, at whatever level, planning, preparation, resources, and execution or implementation are vital. You might have to spend money and call in the IOUs people owe you. You might have to drop just about everything else you're doing to achieve victory or avoid defeat. But if the issue is indeed important, there's no sense fighting with one hand and the other tied behind your back while your opponent is using both hands and both feet. Your goal is to accomplish your objectives using your skills, power, and resources as is appropriate to the type of conflict you're engaged in. You should try to get a reputation that if you are attacked (unfairly or otherwise), you will negotiate if that seems reasonable, but you will also fight very hard and very tough (within the bounds of decency). Internal and external opponents should know that they run some significant risks if they become involved in a battle with you, but at the same time, if you are wrong you are willing to have a truce and negotiate the issues.

At the same time that you want to be perceived as strong, you also want others to know that you don't act irrationally but will suit your actions to the situation, and that you will strive to avoid defeat or achieve victory, while fighting within the rules. You may want to win and to win decisively, but you should try to avoid totally humiliating your internal opponents. If you do, they or their colleagues may bear very long, lasting grudges that can hurt you and ultimately lead to a successful quest for revenge. Depending on the situation, you may want to avoid humiliating your external opponent for the same reason.

Fortunately, management issues are rarely of the magnitude of the approach used here of war and peace. However, some issues, strategies, tactics, or operating styles may be of crucial importance to your company, to your unit, and to you. In those cases, it is reasonable and wise for you to look at the matter as analogous to a battle and for you to apply logic, toughness, and mercy.

15

INTEGRITY AND INVOLVEMENT

I have been fortunate to have worked for and with some outstanding executives. Their skill levels, positions, ages, personalities, and managerial styles varied. They were quite different, but what they had in common led me to believe that there was a simple "I" test that was critical to the success of truly outstanding managers.

The first "I," and perhaps the fundamental basis for the highest levels of continual management success, is integrity. These individuals possessing integrity can be trusted in word and action, in planning and implementation, in professional and personal dealings, to hold to the highest standards. Their word and their handshake are as strong as a 100-page legal document and several escrow accounts. You can bank and commit resources based on their assurance to you and know that to the extent that is humanly possible, they will deliver what they have said or written. Beyond living up to their commitments, you know through the experience you and others have had with them that they will act with a sense of honor and obligation in their analyses and decisions and their approval of actions to be taken by the unit or company. There are no double standards, no overlooking certain things, or winks, or coverups, or Watergates. There is the sense of highest integrity in dealing with peers, superiors, and subordinates, with customers, clients, the broader community, competitors, and suppliers. And they have not only personal integrity, but a desire to inculcate those standards in their unit and company so that all operate under principles of honesty and concern for the "right" way of doing things, both in spirit and in letter. One can be a moral person without being a moralist; one can be practical yet idealistic in terms of high standards of conduct. By precept and practice that sense of honor, of exemplary standards, can uplift an entire organization.

The other part of the "I" test is involvement—getting involved personally and committed to the mundane as well as the magnificent aspects of the work to be done and seeing to it that as far as possible and as low down in the organization as possible, others are provided the ways and means to become involved in the goals, triumphs, and anguish of the organization. The organization's leaders are seen as being involved with staff, customers, and community.

The employees in the organization believe that they as human beings and as employees count and their satisfaction and security matter to the leaders. There is thus a commitment within the organization to seeking, listening, and reacting to ideas, suggestions, and reactions of all levels of employees before, during, after actions are taken. There is a sense that people will be informed and committed and that their views and the impact of actions on them will be among the major criteria by which alternatives are evaluated. And that all of this is for real—management is not merely adopting the latest thinking in participative management, Theory Z, or Quality Circle approaches. There is a basic trust of employees' brains and ideas rather than a view of them as just bodies, backs, or resources; and there is a concern for feelings, sensitivities, aspirations, and values of those involved with the organization.

The outstanding leaders seek this dual aspect of involvement—their involvement in the company and with its people, while at the same time they encourage and create an appropriate climate for employee involvement in the objectives and goals of the organization, with each other, and with their supervisors and executives of the organization.

There's a great deal to management and one must be careful not to latch on to a few key words that purport to sum it all up. But, if you have to begin focusing on something first as you increase your knowledge, experience, and responsibility, the "I" test isn't a bad way to start.

16

THE MENTOR RELATIONSHIP: (1) FIND A MENTOR; (2) YOUR "CHILDREN" AND "DISCIPLES" GROW UP—LET THEM GO!

To those who desire to advance quickly, a valuable step is finding a mentor, the right mentor. By a mentor, we mean a person (usually older) in a more powerful position (the higher the better) who will serve as a counselor, friend, and adviser. Ideally, your mentor serves to help you get better assignments and rise in the organization or helps you get good positions in other organizations. Sometimes, the potential mentor will seek you out after assessing you as having great potential or because he or she likes you; sometimes you will have to plan carefully which mentor to select and how to cultivate a relationship with this person.

One can't just go up to a division head, vice-president, or president and ask, "Will you be my mentor?" You may have worked for the individual on a particular project, pleased him or her, and felt very comfortable in your working relationship. You may have heard good things about this person: "He's a good guy and a rising star," "she develops people well," and comments such as these. But if you haven't had exposure to the individual or done something he or she would notice, you have to plan how to get noticed. The person may be active in an organization or activity within the company or in the community, and you should then become involved in these and, thus, create interaction. This could be anything from playing racquetball together to working on community chest committees. You can try to get assigned to task forces this person is heading. You might consider sending the individual a memo on something you know is of interest to him or her or just arrange an appointment to talk together about a certain subject, indicating that you wish to become involved. The latter approaches are somewhat unusual and a bit risky, but remember, your goal is to create an opportunity to be noticed. It may take many months or a few years to establish a true mentor relationship, but it is worth the effort. One can have more than one mentor in the company, but that is somewhat difficult to manage. It really depends on the depth of the relationship, the levels of the mentors within the company, and their relationship with each other. At times, there may be a co-worker who is not going to rise much higher but takes pride in helping a younger person succeed. You may indeed leave him or her far behind as you reach for the top, but the individual may have helped you at the start and may remain a trusted counselor thereafter.

The individual who has a mentor is not just a taker, using the mentor to get ahead. He or she is giving something to the mentor. For many people, at various stages of their careers, there is a strong desire to help others learn, grow, and succeed. This desire may stem from feelings about wanting to pass on their knowledge and thus strengthen and perpetuate their impact on the unit, company, or industry. Or, they wish to groom potentially strong allies, their successor, or someone to advance higher than they did. Or, they may develop a personal and emotional bond to the individual seeking their help so that they are like a father or uncle, wanting to do everything possible to prepare the individual and help pave the way to success. There is considerable satisfaction in seeing their professional "son" or "daughter"—their "disciple"—do well because of the guidance they have given and opportunities they have provided. At the same time, the talented person who has loyalty to them may be a great help in their own careers and may well fulfill a need they may have to teach and develop others.

There comes a point, however, when the "child" is ready and eager to go out on his or her own. For many mentors, the situation is similar to that of parents whose grown children leave home and strike out on their own, or advance faster in their careers than the father and mother, perhaps even surpassing them. There comes a time when even though the personal relationship is still important, the disciple no longer needs the mentor. He or she has learned all that can be taught, is climbing alone, and no longer needs a push or help of any kind. He or she may, in fact, even outdistance the mentor on the way up, leaving the guide either standing still or on the way down. For the mentor, there is both pride in observing the accomplishments and sadness in noting that he or she is no longer needed or not needed as much. The wise mentor will recognize the changed situation and will not attempt to continue the same patterns that existed, but will rather wait for his or her new "colleague" to demonstrate independence and to indicate how the relationship should proceed. The acceptance of one's former student as a peer is a difficult task for the teacher, but out of that acceptance can come a new relationship that is beneficial and rewarding to both.

17

IT PAYS TO CARE

We have emphasized the "Mr. Cool" approach in American management. We're calm, cool, and collected. We do things by the numbers, quantify the unquantifiable, and place our trust in computer printouts and terminals. We keep our emotions in check and deal with human concerns as little as possible. We worry—if we do something special for Joe, are we setting a dangerous precedent?

I suggest that both in the short and long run it pays to care, to care deeply, about our organization and our unit, and the people in them. This sense of caring for the organization as an institution, as an ongoing concern, as something that is good and getting better and that is making an important contribution in what it does and how it does it, gives a broader purpose to the organization and the people in it. We're all working for something more than just a paycheck, a bonus, and our pensions. We're working to make our unit and company better and the best. This does not mean we need pep rallies and company songs (although those ideas aren't necessarily bad). But we need to have a sense that the unit and company are bigger than we are; that not only must we recognize the importance of how it does now but we need also to think in terms of laying a solid foundation for the future. We need to indicate a sense of history of the organization, of its accomplishments, innovations, and the contributions of particular individuals at all levels.

While trying to instill caring by staff for the organization as an entity, the organization also must care about its reputation, its standards of quality and service, and the services and support it gives to the community.

Of particular importance is the sense of caring, both on the part of the organization toward its employees and on the part of each individual, one to another. In a sense, the goal is to create a feeling of belonging, of an extended family. In huge corporations, this is difficult to do, but it can be started at the smallest unit level. By company policies and practices, by traditions that units and presidents start and adhere to, one can demonstrate concern for staff members as individuals. If there has been a calamity in one's life or a joyous occasion, it should matter to one's fellow employees, and at least to the unit, if not the division or company as a whole. It does matter that one has done something on or off the job that is important, or that one is ill. It does matter to fellow employees that one needs help in some way, or that someone who has been retired or laid off has not been forgotten.

It doesn't take much money or time to let our instincts as human beings extend to the workplace and for the organization to encourage and support social interaction on and off the job. It does, however, take a desire to depart from usual practices and a willingness to be in the forefront of humanizing the workplace.

The payoff is rather obvious. It is important to have a sense of loyalty and dedication to each other, the unit, and the company, and to have a deep concern about what happens to us as individuals, as staff members, and to our home away from home. This concern is very likely to be translated into a stable and satisfied workforce and increased productivity, creativity, profits, and attractiveness to potential employees and to the community in which the firm is located.

18

YOU'VE GOTTA BELIEVE

We all experience moments, days, weeks, and sometimes months when we get down on ourselves and others. We may have problems in our lives such as the death of a loved one, a poor or failing marriage, divorce, illness, problems with children, boredom, too much to handle, financial concerns, and the mountain of problems and disappointments we all face. Sometimes, these are of such importance and quantity in a short time period that they would overwhelm and depress any person, thick-skinned or not. The same may be true of your professional life—goofs or mistakes by you or others, a raise or promotion not granted, competitors or colleagues outshining you, boredom, burnout, too much pressure, too much to do, no light at the end of the tunnel, too much of the same old thing, and on and on.

Problems in the nonwork sector of your life may spill over and affect the work sector (or vice versa) or make you less able to cope with problems in the other and, thus, the problems may feed on and multiply each other. It is possible that the problems will cause a mild to severe case of depression and you may find it extremely difficult to fight your way out of it by yourself, even assuming that you have the strength or desire to wage the fight. It is very easy and natural in these situations to lose faith and hope in yourself.

With effort, you can overcome the situation and build a foundation to cope with similar situations that arise in the future. First, you must try to objectively analyze the causes of your feelings of depression or your sense of being a failure, that life isn't fun or worth living. If you can isolate the reasons and causes, you can at least stare the sources of discomfort in the face rather than just dealing with a dark cloud. You can then try to see how important and longlasting these things are. Is it a temporary condition or one that is going to last for a long time? You may hate your boss, but maybe he or she is going to retire, be promoted, transferred, or fired. Perhaps you can transfer. You may hate your job, but there is nowhere to go in the company and the job market is lousy. Or, you may have to keep saying, This too shall pass.

After knowing what it is that's troubling you and the nature and magnitude of the condition, you then can seek to explore ways to deal with the situation—what you can do yourself, what help you need from others. Developing a plan to deal with the problem, even if the plan does not succeed, at least provides the comfort of knowing you are taking action and are not helpless. In most cases, you will need help in dealing with the problem, even if that help is only the sympathetic ear of a loved one, friend, or mentor. In other cases, you will need the professional help of a counselor, psychologist, or psychiatrist. (It may be wise to get a medical checkup because there may be a physical problem that is causing or aggravating the psychological problem.) It is important to understand when you are unable to deal with the issues yourself despite your best efforts and thus need the help of others. Why suffer needlessly and longer than you should if, through various types of talking out, counseling, and therapy, you can be helped?

If you can also remember how you've conquered other problems, handled your previous successes, and if you can, your previous good feelings about yourself as you meet various problems that arise you will have the foundation and incentive to deal with the current situation. In regard to your professional problem, you may want to go through the exercise of writing a long letter of recommendation about yourself or a detailed resumé. Don't be modest, but don't kid yourself. As you see what you have accomplished in the face of difficulty and adversity, you may begin to realize once again that you are pretty good! In many cases, believing in yourself as a professional and as a person—I've done good things, I've done it before and will do it again, I am good and getting better—will provide the basis for your conquering the problems you face.

At the same time that you build and strengthen belief in yourself, you need to convey to others these feelings in themselves. Colleagues, superiors, subordinates, and others in the organization who know that you believe in them and have faith, trust, and confidence in them as human beings and as professionals will reciprocate that feeling and, thus, reinforce your own good feelings about yourself. In addition, their good feelings about themselves will influence their performance, their ability to meet adversity, and their willingness to confide in you. One can believe in others and still expect and demand high performance, rewarding and punishing as necessary. But confidence and trust between people will serve to motivate others and to build an atmosphere and climate in the organization that is a powerful force in making the organization and those in it successful.

19

THERE'S MORE TO LIFE THAN WORK

As we all strive to reach our goals in our organization, profession, and career, it is valuable to pause from time to time to take stock of the totality of our lives. We may indeed be on the fast track to job success but on a very slow track in terms of satisfaction beyond the job.

Many of us, particularly the high achievers, get so wrapped up in the pursuit of the fame, fortune, power, and prestige connected with career advancement and success of the organization that we don't critically evaluate ourselves and our lives as separate from our careers. Sometimes, of course, it can be a cop-out—I didn't get the vice presidency or presidency so I'll concentrate on family, friends, community organizations, hobbies, and so on, or, I am a person who has wide interests and concerns for family; thus, I am not willing to sacrifice everything to the job and that's why I wasn't promoted to . . .

The point is, there can be a balance between one's work life and life beyond the office, but at times you have to focus on whether there's more to you and to your life than your office, title, and company. It would be helpful for you to evaluate yourself, based on per month activities, by asking such questions as:

- How much time do I spend with my spouse alone and in social situations?
- How much time do I spend with my children alone, in family, and in social situations?
- How much time do I spend with family and friends, alone and in social situations?
- Are my friends and those I interact with socially different from those in my organization or line of work?
- What do I do when I am not in the office? How much time is spent during my "off" hours on business-related activities? On non-business-related activities?
- What are my hobbies and interests other than my job, company, industry, or profession and how much time do I spend on them?
- If I were given a month off and not allowed to work, what would I do with my time? How much do I think I would enjoy what I was doing?
- If I were given 3 months, 6 months, or 12 months off from work, what would I do? How much do I think I would enjoy it?
- What do I usually do evenings? Saturdays? Sundays? Holidays? What would I really like to do?
- What contributions of time, energy, and thought have I made to my neighborhood, community, civic, athletic, cultural, or religious organizations?
- If I were invited to a cocktail party and the ground rules were that no one could discuss his or her job or anyone else's job, would I go? What would I like to talk about? What would I like to learn from others?
- What do I read? How often?
- What do I watch on television? How often?
- When I really want to feel good about life or feel good about myself, what do I do?

- What's a good time to me?
- What's a great weekend?
- What's a great vacation?
- What do I feel deeply about?

There are no "right" answers to any of these questions and you can easily expand the list. What you should be trying to do is ascertain how interesting and interested a person are you, not so much to others, but to yourself. Are you pleased with the picture that emerges from the frank answers to the questions?

My own view is that each of us needs outlets and changes from the pace and type of activities we engage in on our jobs and that these different activities, involvements, concerns, and commitments are very important. Many are important, not because we should each seek to be a well-rounded person, but because we can get our satisfaction and kicks from a variety of sources—the more sources of satisfaction (or the more deeply fewer sources are pursued), the more likely we are to be a happier, more complete person. If all you've got is a job and title, no matter how important or well-paid, you are, in fact, a relatively poor person. The power and position of today may be short-lived in the face of mergers, acquisitions, new bosses, or organizational frameworks. Even if you enjoy your work for many years, there will be a phase-out period as you get older. Will you wait until then to become close to family and friends or to develop interests and concerns? It may be too late. Even in the prime of your career, non-work involvement can provide satisfaction, change of pace, interests, and outlets that give you a zest for life, that make your life and indeed your work more enjoyable. It is difficult to recognize that practically no one is indispensable. Once you realize that, you can begin to focus on being and becoming, for yourself and others, more than manager of _____ , vice president for _____ , president.

20

Work Can Be Fun—Laugh, Relax, Enjoy

When was the last time you received a funny memo or note while at work, heard a joke or quip during a meeting, heard solid laughter, were part of a prank, saw twinkles in people's eyes and grins on their faces? If you are able to honestly say such things happen fairly frequently, you should be grateful. Most organizations are rather uptight. There's not enough fun and relaxation in the workplace. If we are able to change that and introduce a greater sense of relaxation, happiness, and laughter, we will create an atmosphere that is more conducive to job and personal satisfaction, loyalty to the company, and a greater degree of motivation and productivity.

By fun, I don't mean storytelling time each day, or a series of pranks and counterpranks, but rather an atmosphere where humor is not frowned on, where people can see the lighter side in tense situations, where a serious meeting can be introduced with the latest joke someone heard (if the story or time seems appropriate), where a funny note or memo can defuse a hot situation or just demonstrate that one has a funny bone and sense of the ridiculous.

Of course, there are some people who really don't have a sense of humor or have a terrible one, or who can't tell or appreciate a funny incident or story if their lives were to depend on it. All one can hope is that the whole organization isn't like that.

A good sense of humor and sense of timing as to when to use it can be very helpful as part of one's leadership style, in building group feeling and personal relationships. It demonstrates an aspect of the person and the organization that can serve to make people feel there are real, breathing human beings around, people with personalities as well as brains and ambition.

Good managers will encourage appropriate use of a light approach as long as it does not get out of hand or detract from accomplishing the unit's goals, because they know it can build a sense of comfort on the job that significantly improves individuals' feelings about their colleagues, unit, and organization, as well as about themselves. You, as an individual, have to be careful not to overdo humor, especially if people seem to like your delivery. After all, you are not expected to be a stand-up comic, and the danger of always saying something funny is that you will condition others to look for that rather than the substance of what you are saying.

The organization and manager should strive to create an atmosphere that recognizes the need for people to have a sense of enjoying themselves and occasionally laughing at situations, the world, and themselves, while also emphasizing the importance of developing and reaching goals. If you are able to do so, you will have a significant advantage over those who, in effect, discourage humor, relaxation, and enjoyment.

21

WHEN YOU KNOCK ON YOUR DOOR, IS THERE ANYONE HOME?

There comes a time, often several times, in your and everyone else's career and life when you need to take stock of yourself. Despite the title, salary, performance record, and impressive resumé, who and what are you? This is not a question to be asked merely at a time of mid-career crisis, or when evaluating yourself after you've been fired, passed over for a big promotion, have really screwed up, are about to retire, or are having serious family problems. Those events may occasion a somewhat tension-filled need for looking into yourself. However, it is wise to do so on a regular basis, perhaps every several years or possibly every year, at around New Year's, when many people are in the mood to make resolutions and evaluate results on previous resolutions. (If such evaluations are to be meaningful, it might be best not to take one's "temperature" too often, although one might be tempted to be deeply introspective semiannually, quarterly, or even monthly.)

Many of us get caught up in the race for success and in winning as many victories as possible that we don't stop to think why we are running at all and what our personal goals are beyond more power, responsibility, prestige, financial success, and security. Once you're reached certain goals, what do you do for an encore? What difference does it really make when you're at the top—to you, to your family, to your organization? This does not mean that life, challenge, and success have no meaning and we should all hand in our attaché cases and personal computers and dig clams on the beach. What it does mean is that in terms of ourselves as human beings first and managers second, it is important to know and question ourselves, to be comfortable with Joe Smith as an individual first, rather than with Joe Smith, successful executive.

Knowing oneself provides the basis for understanding, for relating to others and to issues within the organization and external to it, for relating to the community and world around us. It provides the basis for being able to deal with the vicissitudes of life and career, of meeting the joys and sadness that face all of us, of dealing with success and failure, and with life after one's career has topped out or when we face retirement. Most of us will live, depending upon the age of retirement, 10 to 20 years after "retiring." The quality of that rather lengthy period may very well depend on the tuning in on oneself that has occurred and the action taken in response, many years before retirement.

It may come down to what pleases you and what do you hope to accomplish on and off the job? What kind of person do you really want to be? What do you want family and friends, as well as professional colleagues, to really think of you during your working career and after you have left a particular organization for another or for retirement? What do you want to be remembered for when you're no longer a full-time employee or no longer alive? When you begin to think in those terms, your questions, answers, and actions may be quite different from what you've thought or done before.

The focus has been on others' reactions to you. But more important is your reaction to you. How do you want to think of yourself, realistically and objectively, and what changes or courses of action do you have to take to reach fulfillment of your self-image? Forget for a moment pleasing others or living up to expectations—what are your expectations for yourself and how do you get to live up to them? As an executive, you know how to define objectives and develop plans for meeting them. Do that for yourself. Look closely at the basic you. Learn and commit yourself to do those things that make you proud of yourself as a person, that lead you to be strong friends with the inner you, to look and enjoy the inner you.

Perhaps the most important thing you can ever do and your greatest and probably toughest challenge is reaching your goals as a person. This may be undertaken through short, serious introspection and, if necessary, as you see it, concerted effort. If you need something to get you going in terms of looking at yourself, just remember that "today is the first day of the rest of your life."

22

GROW A REASONABLY THICK SKIN

Sensitivity to other people, or to issues, conditions, or nuances is a valuable asset. Oversensitivity about yourself, your work, and unit, or to the previously cited factors can be detrimental to your success. The difficult question is, how do you strike a balance between sensitivity and oversensitivity? It is important not to be so aloof and nonreactive to what's happening that you turn people off and lack the ability to take decisive action when necessary. On the other hand, you don't want to overreact, make everything into a critical issue, and act as if you're bleeding profusely and your life is in danger when all you have suffered is a slight cut. Those with very thin skins feel injured much too quickly and react too often, rapidly, and forcefully. Those with very thick skins don't react often enough or in the appropriate fashion.

Most people are more likely to have a too-thin skin rather than a too-thick one. This is particularly true early in your career when you have not yet acquired the experience, skills, and reputation that give you the self-confidence to handle real and perceived slings and arrows as well as the minor and major disasters that you are bound to face. It may be helpful, therefore, for you to think about some techniques or approaches that seek to maintain the advantage of being sensitive while lessening the consequences of being too sensitive—in short, how to grow a somewhat thicker skin.

First, don't personalize too many things. People can and will find your views disagreeable while still liking and respecting you. An attack on your views or work product is not necessarily an attack on you as a person or an insult to your intelligence, work habits, and dedication.

Second, recognize that nobody is perfect. You or your unit may have indeed goofed or committed a major blunder or may have had a bad day, week, or month; be grateful if the response is relatively mild and merciful and learn as much as you can about what caused the goof or error and how you can prevent the same and similar mistakes from happening in the future. Admit there was an error, take responsibility, apologize. Don't try to stonewall or cast too many stones at others. Take your lumps and go on to other things. Don't keep recalling and reliving your errors and defeats.

Third, learn how to close the door on an issue or how to take it off the table and put it away. Too many people keep worrying about the errors they made months or years ago and assume that the current situation will end up similar to a previous bad one. Why not assume it will end up similar to a previous success? Even if there's another mistake, you should avoid linking it to a pattern of errors, because presumably you have learned from past failures. Even if the same problem occurs again, learn from it but don't keep coming back to it consciously or unconsciously. Once an issue is decided, don't try to keep redeciding it.

Fourth, remember the child's rhyme, "Sticks and stones will break my bones but words will never hurt me." There's some truth to that except that some words may hurt you personally in terms of your ego and self-esteem and others will hurt your reputation. But try if you can to let the gratuitous insult roll off your back and keep a stiff upper lip about the others. Learn from the comments, but try not to let them wound you too deeply or too long. (Other parts of the book will indicate how you can counterattack.)

Fifth, enjoy but don't flaunt your successes and learn from them. Don't brood over your defeats, yet learn from them.

Sixth, when you are down on yourself or your unit, remember the good things that have happened, and why, as a counterbalance to the bad.

Seventh, try to understand why others may be taking pot shots at you. It may have nothing to do with your work effort or yourself. They may be under particular work or family pressures, may not feel well, may be jealous of you, may feel threatened by you, or have other difficulties of this nature.

By growing a thicker skin you will be able to avoid being overly hurt by or reacting strongly to those things that are really just bruises, nicks, or small cuts, and you will also be able to handle better the really major blows. It will take time and effort to thicken your skin, but the effort is worth it because you will become a more effective manager.

23

NOBODY'S PERFECT!

———— ✳✳✳✖✳✳✳ ————

It's important to set high standards of performance for yourself and your subordinates and to evaluate results in a tough but fair manner. However, as we strive to be as good as we possibly can, to beat the competition and our goals, to pitch the "perfect" game, we must recognize that nobody's perfect.

The point is, you have to understand that you, your superiors, colleagues, peers, and subordinates are going to make mistakes, wrong decisions, errors of omission and commission, and simply blow some. Obviously, this applies not only to work. The President of the United States, the Chief Justice of the Supreme Court, your clergyman, your parents, spouse, and children, and, alas, the writer of this book, are also not perfect.

Learning to live with mistakes and poor, even terrible, decisions and actions made by you and others is an important aspect of being a successful manager and in leading a reasonably calm life. This does not mean one should overlook major errors or shrug them off. It does mean that we have to understand that they will occur. In baseball, for example, hitting .400 is almost impossible, and hitters who hit .333 are considered excellent. Consider what that means. If someone has a career batting average of .333, he is likely to get into the Hall of Fame. But that simply says he got a hit one third of the time, and the very, very rare .400 hitter only got a hit 40 percent of the time. The professional basketball player who makes 65 percent of his shots is considered outstanding, and a basketball coach would be very pleased if the team made 55 percent of its shots.

Once we begin to understand that various degrees of errors will occur, from simple goofs or "I forgots" to colossal or calamitous blunders, we can then focus on learning from the errors and dealing with them. For ourselves and others, it is important to do a post mortem examination on the major mistakes. Why did they occur? What breakdowns in communication, analysis, planning, information, execution of plans, follow-up, and so on caused them? What can we do now to control the damage or bring the situation under control? In regard to preventing future errors, what procedural or policy changes, training and development, improved methods of analysis, communication, planning, information gathering, and so on are necessary? What improved methods of monitoring, control, or evaluation are necessary? For mistakes that range from relatively minor to important, one can follow the same approach as indicated above and adjust it depending on the nature and importance of the error. For very minor and very infrequent goofs, it is probably best to forget them.

The most important thing about "nobody's perfect" is to fully accept that you and others are human, and to be forgiving of yourself and others. At the same time, we ought to be learning and growing from our failures, and to be learning as much as we can about the situation and the elements within ourselves that caused the problem, so that we can take corrective action and lessen the chances for the same type of error happening in the future. For yourself and others, you should be concerned whether the same kind of error is being repeated. It is better to have five different kinds of mistakes than five mistakes of the same kind. In order to get a better batting average in decisions or actions (33 percent to 65 percent is not acceptable in management—with those batting/scoring averages one not only doesn't get into the Hall of Fame, one doesn't get into the office any longer), one must know about the errors, analyze why they happened, and take corrective action for the present and future. This may include taking various types of courses and training experiences; making notes to improve your memory; modifying your operating style; improving your use of time, concentration, attention to detail, and information flow; developing subordinates; reviewing resource allocations, delegation, supervisory techniques, the authority one has, the organizational structure, and planning system; and so on. It may also be that a person is burned out or needs a vacation or a modification in assignment.

Perhaps making mistakes is the best learning device, but at advancing rungs of the success ladder one expects to have decreasing education through that means. One must be wise enough to know that though one has been burned by and learned from a particular situation, the new situation one faces may not be exactly the same as the previous one. Thus, one has to be careful not to make the mistake of acting in such a manner so as to avoid a previously committed mistake, only to find it is not relevant to the present situation.

As we strive for greater success, we must have the humility and humanity to recognize people's fallibility as well as their capacity to learn, grow, and improve themselves.

24

THINK BEFORE YOU SPEAK

The mind can retain and store a great deal of material, more than most of us imagine. As experiments and people cross-examined under hypnosis demonstrate, various images are imprinted on our brains without our even being conscious of what is happening. Through natural capacity, experience, and various memory and retention techniques, we are relatively effective information storage and handling units. Under the right conditions, we can search our memory banks, just as a computer does, and come up with a good deal of information. But even though we can, do we want to or need to?

My point is simply that in order to use time and concentration power effectively so that we delve into, remember, store, and retrieve what is really important, we ought to be as discriminating as we can in what we want to store in our memory banks. We certainly can fill our heads with a great deal of material, but why bother with junk? The more junk we have in our memory, the more likely we are to mix up what is important. Thus, in going through reports, facts, analyses, and various reading matter, decide what should immediately go into the wastebasket; what can be dealt with quickly and in a skimming-over fashion; what's important for careful reading; what's of considerable importance meriting careful attention and follow-up questions; and, finally, what's of critical importance that you may have to read several times and immediately enter into your memory bank. In this way, you are spending time and thought and your memory capacity on the important things; when situations arise you have sufficient depth of knowledge and attention to detail so that you can utilize the information quickly and accurately. The ability to commit the important to memory is a valuable asset in your work and also is very impressive to others.

Related to the use of your brainpower is the idea of knowing when to speak up and when to be quiet. Often people speak up too soon, too often, or in a tone or manner that is objectionable to others. Furthermore, they may have very little of substance to say but just want to show that they are involved, have views, are intelligent, witty, and articulate. This should be weighed against the danger of creating an impression of not having anything to say, of not being intelligent, or of lacking interest. Those experienced in management recognize that it is better to be known as a person of relatively few words who expresses them succinctly, in a well-thought-out, articulate manner, geared to hitting the center of the target, rather than the verbose, scattershot, off-center speaker.

If you have time to prepare for a meeting, it is good to get the facts about the issues that are on the agenda or are likely to come up and think through your position on the various items. Then, when the appropriate opportunity arises, you say your piece, modified by whatever new information has come out or by views expressed at the meeting. On a good number of issues, you don't have time to prepare. You have to rely on your memory bank and general knowledge. But you should also develop the capacity of being a good listener who concentrates on what is said, by whom, how, the reactions to and by others, and the body language and facial expressions of the others at the meeting. These impressions can help you formulate, quickly, the content and style of your response. Furthermore, how you say what you want to say is important—the tone, choice of words, and body language. And generally, you don't want to take potshots at those whose viewpoints or manner you disagree with. You can praise what you agree with and even the soundness or reasonableness of opposing viewpoints, and then go on to try to convince others by building on the strengths and pointing out the weaknesses of previously expressed viewpoints. In this way, you build support for your own viewpoint by showing how others have contributed. Sometimes you will be the originator of the idea, sometimes the compiler or synthesizer. In taking the approach outlined, you can have a major impact on the discussion and on decision making.

Equally important is making sure you have thought things through before you send a memo or letter. If it is a controversial topic, read your draft very carefully several times, preferably at different times of the day, and if possible, on different days. Your emotions may have taken hold of you and you may end up deeply regretting what you have written in haste, under stress, tension, or tiredness, or out of anger. Read the memo from the point of view of the receiver—your boss, other colleagues. Will they think the points you have made are well reasoned, clearly stated, and reasonably and logically presented, even if they disagree with your approach or conclusions? Have you substituted anger for facts, personal dislike for cool analysis? It may be helpful to wait a day on your most important memos before sending them so that you can read them again the next day. Certainly, you should read your nasty memos (and we all write some of these) again when you are not angry, even if it is a day or two later. In almost all cases, you will find that you will want to tone down the memos, destroy them, or file them in the file marked Memos I Wanted to Send, But Wisely Didn't.

What you say, how, and when can raise you to great heights or lower you to the bottom or out of the organization. The same is true of what you write, but that can come back to haunt you even faster. Thus, use your brain, harness your emotions, and make sure your brain is in gear before your tongue and pen are in motion.

25

YOUR GUARDIAN ANGEL

It is comforting to believe that you have a guardian angel who somehow helps you succeed or, at least, prevents you from making terrible errors in judgment or action. Some call this a "sixth sense," "intuition," "a feeling in my gut," "a red, yellow, or green light flashing." Such a belief, valid or invalid, can be helpful to your self-confidence and willingness to take risks.

I believe that through experience and training, many individuals can develop a warning system that can be helpful in reducing the risks in decision making and action. Some people do this by making checklists of what to look for; using various decision making, problem solving, and analytical techniques; probing issues and people through penetrating questions; carefully developing and evaluating subordinates; evaluating colleagues; developing and using management information systems; recognizing that the time is not right for making a major decision or that their psychological, physical, or emotional state is not right for making a decision at this time (they may be "high" or "low"). Others may not need some or any of these approaches, but through experience and intuition just get a sense that something is not quite right and, thus, take no action on the problem until they spend more time on it and isolate the reason for their discomfort. They then can see to it that the issue is studied further, using various techniques or, at least, that a final decision is put off for a while until more thought is given, information and analysis developed, or the heated atmosphere of the moment cools down a bit.

As a manager, I believe in rational, analytical approaches, but I also believe in tuning in and trusting your guardian angel or intuition. If your guardian angel is buzzing, you should hold off for awhile, even after analysis says "go." Believe in your angel . . . but not too much! There is danger in going overboard on this and in believing that your angel is always with you or is always needed. You may end up delaying things dangerously long while waiting for your guardian angel to let you go ahead.

On the other hand, if you believe in your angel's protection too deeply, and you act upon this too much, you may fall prey to taking very bad risks or making decisions too quickly on the assumption that because you're a good or lucky person, protected by your guardian angel, you cannot fail.

If you listen to your angel and things turn out wrong, don't cast aside your feeling of intuition. Be understanding, and assume your angel was on vacation, or tired, and was not working overtime. Believe that your angel is still available to be of assistance, if used carefully and moderately.

26

PERCEPTIONS ARE AS IMPORTANT AS REALITY

Managers can learn something from politicians, and that is the importance of other people's perceptions. Good politicians are masters at presenting things in such a way that the substance and style create a favorable impression for the content of what the president, senator, congressman, or governor is saying or doing as well as for him or her as an individual. While learning this lesson, managers should be aware of the danger of overemphasizing perceptions. For example, sometimes politicians overdo the image and worry more how it "plays" in a particular region, city, or neighborhood, or are more concerned about the one-day deadline or sixty-second television story than whether it is indeed a good idea, will work, or has worked. Unfortunately, the media support the possibility of government-by-press-release by giving more prominent space and time to the announcement of exciting concepts, plans and services, wrongdoings, and mistakes, than to evaluation of what happened to the plans a year or two later.

It is valuable when developing plans for changes, new products, plant relocations, staff layoffs or dismissals, recall of products, new organizational arrangements, and so on, to focus on how this action will be perceived by various audiences. You have to be careful to be as objective as possible and separate how you want people to view something, or how they should view it, from how they are likely to view it from their perspective. This involves being able to put yourself into other people's heads and shoes, and it may take some time to get a real sense of how others will view your action or announcement. It becomes particularly difficult when you have more than one important audience, and one group is likely to look at things one way and the other another way. For important announcements by an organization, depending upon the subject matter, the audiences may be one or more of the following: employees, stock- and bond-holders, customers, suppliers, government officials, community members and leaders, trade association officials, competitors, stockbrokers and investment firms, the media.

What is said, how, when, where, by whom, the form or forms of the communication, all are important factors in creating the reaction you wish. It is often helpful to consider clarity and simplicity, the thoughts or questions that are most likely to be raised, and how what you said might be misinterpreted or twisted. Some announcements, for instance, layoffs or plant closings, are emotionally searing to individuals and a community, and extra-careful consideration must be given to these types of announcements.

I have talked about major company-wide actions, but in everything one does, at every level, perceptions are important: Why doesn't he answer my telephone calls? What did she mean by that cryptic remark? Why is my performance evaluation delayed? Why didn't he explain what he wanted? I don't understand what she means. Our budget has been reduced . . . my boss seems distracted . . . why was he and not I invited to dinner by the boss . . . why did she and not others get more space, equipment, a new rug . . . why didn't I get . . . ?

Of course, you want to spend your efforts on the reality of a situation, on making the right things happen, on ensuring accuracy and the accomplishment of goals. But, all along the way, be careful to keep asking yourself in all that you do or plan to do, How will the various audiences assess what I am doing and saying, and how can I present things in an accurate, informative, and favorable light?

27

You Can't Take It with You

In the scope of any job, there are things one likes to do better than others. Some aspects of the job give a great deal of personal and professional satisfaction and a sense of great expertise and outstanding accomplishment. Thus, when one is promoted, it is natural to want to take with one those things you enjoy greatly, if possible. The rationale is, "I'm truly excellent at this and I really enjoy it." Although some promotions would allow and even require such carrying forward of responsibilities, generally you expect the higher level position to require knowledge and oversight of the functions performed at a lower level, but not the same degree of "hands on" effort. One is generally not promoting an individual to spend more time with his or her past activities, but to spend less time and take on new or additional responsibilities and a somewhat or largely different perspective. Although the individual feels comfortable, happy, and expert at the old job and may feel uncomfortable, tense, and inexperienced at the new one, the newly promoted person and his or her superior should focus on leaving behind most or all of the old responsibilities. This allows you to devote your energies and concern to the new responsibilities, to switch gears and tracks in your thinking. It also allows your successor to have a relatively free hand to learn and grow in his or her new responsibilities, to develop his or her own approach, relying on you when necessary, but without interference.

Another aspect of "you can't take it with you" is that in the long run, you can't take your successful track record and accomplishments with you into your new position. That track record gave you credibility in getting the new position, and you may indeed have made a major and lasting contribution. You are entitled to the acclaim and reward (your promotion) you received, but after a while, when you are mentioned as the person who accomplished "x" on your former job, but without notice of what you have accomplished in your present job, you're in trouble. Old applause and company newspaper clippings last only so long. You have to earn your applause in each job and each year. "What have you done for me lately?" still prevails.

28

YOU'VE GOTTA PAY YOUR DUES

The ambitious high achiever has a reasonably large ego and considerable self-confidence. He or she seeks to prove his or her capabilities, to fly as high and as fast as possible, to work hard, long, and creatively in order to achieve all those high ambitions. The more ambitious, highly trained, and successful the person has been in the past, the loftier his or her aspirations and the shorter the timetable for achieving various rungs on the ladder to success. However, a number of organizations have found that the high achiever (exemplified by the recently minted holder of an MBA degree with good grades from a good university) is often in too much of a hurry. In essence, such a person wants to be a unit or division manager or vice president much faster than his or her experience and performance would warrant. On the other hand, the highly competent person may feel he or she is being held to a lockstep approach because of tradition or the mediocrity found in the business world.

The point is that those climbing the executive ladder must realize that, normally, one has to pay one's dues. The dues may consist of several years of grounding and exposure in a variety of low-level or relatively unchallenging jobs that may seem to the highly educated and skilled person as well below his or her skill and competency level. "I don't need an MBA for this," is a common complaint. It is often extended to "a college dropout could do this work." An organization will not deliberately waste dollars and talent, but some jobs in whole or in part, particularly at the beginning of one's career, may be boring and unchallenging. Even later in a career, there are aspects of anyone's job that seem to be unimportant or that could be done at a lower level, and other aspects, while performed at the appropriate level, are not particularly stimulating. However, one's performance and attitude in the unexciting or unnoticed areas of corporate life are valuable indicators of performance, flexibility, frustration level, and potential in regard to more challenging assignments.

For those on the lower rungs of the ladder, it is important to pay your dues, in terms of time served in various humdrum jobs, or jobs that are important to the organization, but relatively unrewarding to the individual, with a sense that this apprenticeship is necessary and that you are learning something of value. It is true you may learn what is of value in only a few weeks, while you may have the job many months or several years. However, you should attempt to show that you are approaching your assignment with enthusiasm in the sense that it is part of your growth and orientation and that you can do an outstanding job. You should be able to demonstrate that you have tried to achieve significant innovations and accomplishments and expansions of your functions (and succeeded in your attempts). Of course, you don't want to be overly enthusiastic about an unexciting job; people will think you have reached your level of aspiration! In short, be a good sport about it, learn and contribute as much as you can, recognize that you're paying your dues so that you can advance higher in the organization.

29

ARE YOU PAYING ENOUGH PSYCHIC INCOME?

———— ✹✕✹ ————

For all employees, including those with fabulous compensation packages, there is, in addition to monetary income, another kind of income that is of great importance. It can, with thought and care, be made available to many individuals at all levels in a company from blue-collar worker, to junior executive and on up. This type of income, often overlooked, is what I call psychic income.

Psychic income gives you a sense of the following: fulfillment, ego gratification, self-actualization, realization of one's goals, being held in high regard, being important, doing important things, having significant worth to the company and to oneself, learning, growing, contributing, enjoying what one is doing, making a difference, being creative, making things happen, and developing ideas, products, and people.

A huge compensation package may not guarantee a large psychic income. In fact, some of those who have such packages may be "poor little rich boys (or girls)," because they lack those elements of psychic income that are an increasingly important aspect of feeling good about one's job and one's self, about one's present and future. This element is also increasingly important in the ability of the firm to attract and retain the best and the brightest and in the results achieved by these individuals.

What can be done to improve and increase psychic income will not cost large sums, but it does require commitment and concern about how individuals feel about themselves, their jobs, and their future, and the company. It requires an individual and company environment that is tuned in to psychic income. It requires active concern, involvement, and example, from the president on down, and an indication that a concern for providing psychic income for one's staff is an important element in your performance evaluation.

Here's an easy test to take to determine whether you, as a supervisor or as a high company official, are providing a reasonable amount of psychic income for your subordinates and those in the company. Answer the questions "Always," "Very Frequently," "Fairly Often," "Sometimes," "Rarely," or "Very Rarely or Never."

1. Do you compliment people in writing, orally, at meetings, and in other settings on their accomplishments? (This does not mean just throwing cheap praise around, but complimenting when it is really deserved. If you praise mediocrity, you cheapen the value of praise.)

2. Do you share the limelight and give credit to those who have done the work or come up with the idea?

3. Do you let others present the idea or report, or have their name on the project report or memo, instead of keeping everything in your name?

4. Do you invite your subordinates to important meetings and encourage them to speak up and speak freely?

5. Do you actively encourage and reward people for suggesting things; for their evaluations; for their criticism, creativity, and willingness to depart from the usual and question the status quo?

6. Do you encourage people to disagree with you, to develop and push their own ideas?

7. Do you take time out to have business lunches, coffee, or dinner with subordinates—not just those immediately below you, but further down the line was well?

8. Do you spend some time in small talk with others in order to build rapport and get to know your subordinates—their non-work activities, concerns, and interests?

9. Do you spend some time encouraging others to discuss their goals, ambitions, concerns, and problems with you?

10. Do you discuss opportunities for training, advancement, learning, growth, exposure to new techniques and technology, and attendance at conferences, and see to it that these opportunities become realities for your subordinates?

11. Do you develop opportunities for others for choice assignments, travel, new and challenging projects, and new and challenging responsibilities?

12. Do you introduce your subordinates to top people in the company and give them an opportunity to learn from others, to shine with your boss and his or her boss?

13. Do you give your subordinates the opportunity to fly as high and as fast as they can?

14. When making a decision, an assignment, or an evaluation, do you think: How will this affect the individuals involved and

how, if necessary, can I soften the blow or adequately reward him or her?

15. Do you, in your style and in what you expect of others, emphasize a sense of civility, honesty, openness, and fair play?

16. Do you really care about the individual's feelings, goals, and aspirations?

17. Do you encourage individuals to write or speak about their work or ideas in professional or community organizations, in appropriate journals, in magazines, and in other news media?

18. Do you recognize in some appropriate way outstanding accomplishments not directly related to one's job, such as community activities and civic awards?

19. Do you encourage others to set challenging goals for themselves and their units and do you take an active interest in helping them achieve those goals?

20. Do you see to it that their performance in achieving those tasks or their success on specific projects is recognized in various ways—salary, bonus, praise, recognition in company newspaper, or in other public ways in the company and perhaps outside the company, where appropriate?

Score yourself as follows. For each question you answered:

Always: Score 5 points
Very Frequently: Score 4 points
Fairly Often: Score 3 points
Sometimes: Score 2 points
Rarely: Score 1 point
Very Rarely or Never: Score 0

Total your score. If you scored 85 or above, keep up the good work. You are tuned in and concerned about psychic income and are providing a great deal of this important income to and for your staff; it is to be hoped that you are being treated as well. If the score is 75 to 84, you have a bit of work to do, but you are certainly providing more than adequate psychic income. If the score is between 65 and 74, you are providing adequate psychic income, but improvement is necessary for the good of your employees and the organization. At 55 to 64, you have a considerable amount of work to provide adequate psychic income compensation. With a score of 45 to 54, you have a great deal of work to do; your employees are in a state of deprivation and malnutrition in regard to the income that is so necessary both to the mind and to the heart. Below 44, your employees are in a state of starvation; changing this should become your first priority; you are a terrible scrooge!

By the way, you can apply this test and the scoring to determine how you are being treated. You may have to speak to your supervisor because he or she may have some or even a considerable amount of work to do in meeting your needs. Indeed, you may be suffering from malnutrition or starvation. The only good thing about such suffering is that you get a real sense of how terrible your staff and others feel when they face the same situation.

The way to begin improving is to begin to do or do more often and better the actions implied in the questions and to think about and act on the issue so that you can come up with other ways of providing psychic income geared to your organization. Time, thought, and effort on your part and the change of style and emphasis necessary are very likely to pay huge dividends in terms of job satisfaction for employees (and yourself); lower turnover and absenteeism; greater creativity and productivity; and greater effectiveness, efficiency, and profits for the organization.

Finally, just as we sometimes regret that we never told loved ones who died how much they meant to us, think of what happens when there is a farewell party for someone who is leaving the unit or organization or is retiring. We say honestly and from the heart how much their efforts and their personal characteristics have meant to us and to the unit, even though we often didn't take the time to say it while they were with us. Well, say some of that, honestly, to people at appropriate times during the year and during their career. It will give them immense satisfaction to know they are appreciated and highly regarded as individuals and as workers. In many cases, that kind of psychic income, on a consistent and earned basis, will ensure that people won't leave the organization for greener pastures!

30

Is Anybody Listening—Are You Communicating?

Our ears are bombarded by sounds from TV, radio, cassettes, tapes, telephones, conversations, and lecture platforms. Our eyes are weary from reading the stacks of materials before us. But very often, the new person in the organization or the outside consultant indicates that we have a very serious communication problem. We communicate all the time and sometimes don't know it—for instance, our expression, appearance, gait, sprightliness, posture, tone of voice, or silence.

When we communicate, orally or in writing, we hope to achieve some type of action or reaction, to influence behavior or thought processes. At times, it is more appropriate to reach our audiences in writing, sometimes orally, other times in a combination of ways.

Unfortunately, most organizations stress downward communication, from superiors to subordinates. This is necessary and valuable, but care should be taken about frequency of contact, method of contact, content, clarity, tone, and style.

My major concern is to encourage upward communication—the ability of subordinates to communicate freely and honestly with their superiors. Many supervisors feel if they announce they have an open door policy and require regular reports and exception reports (those that indicate variances from expectations, plans, or budget) from their subordinates, they are indeed encouraging upward communication. In most cases, much more has to be done to bring about an upward communication system that has real value for those transmitting and those receiving the message. As a supervisor, you want to encourage subordinates to communicate bad and good news, and their comments, suggestions, and views. You are concerned about progress, problems, and plans, unusual conditions, and present and potential conflicts. You also want to encourage people to share with you their hopes and fears, feelings and concerns about their work, their future, and the company. If you are able to create a sense of commitment to upward communication, a sense that you really care, that you are listening and thinking about what you are hearing, rather than merely hearing, you will have conquered a major defect in most organizations. In effect, you need an open ear, mind, and heart more than you need an open door.

You should recognize that the organization's complexity, structure, history, and tradition may serve as a barrier to effective upward and two-way communication. You and other supervisors may also be a barrier, since you may be defensive about criticism, feel you don't have the time to communicate often or well, or don't want to get too involved in your subordinates' lives. Subordinates, on the other hand, also have barriers to overcome. They don't have the freedom to interrupt or make demands on their bosses' time; they may fear letting down their guard and telling the whole story rather than just what the boss wants to hear.

Even though there are problems in bringing about better communications, the ways to do so are well known. What is generally lacking is commitment and implementation. Some of the improvements that you can install or encourage include time for one-on-one or group meetings, employee letters, an informative newspaper or newsletter, suggestion systems that work, opportunities for presentation by subordinates, informal conversations at social activities, and the use of attitude surveys and exit interviews. It is also important to regard goal setting and performance review and salary review meetings as valuable communications opportunities.

Poor communications in a unit or organization can be very damaging to individuals and the organization. Commitment, planning, and implementation of an open, honest, upward, and downward communication system can bring about dramatic improvements in morale, climate, and results.

31

THOSE WHO WEAR WELL SUCCEED

Frequently in organizations, newly promoted individuals or new-comers from outside make a decided positive impact on their unit and the company as a whole in a very short period. Their ideas, approaches, motivations, energies, styles, the resources that have been made available to them, the general "honeymoon" period that exists, the things that were waiting to be done, and the enthusiasm they engender in the unit for creativity and improvement—all of these combine to allow them to make their mark. Early success builds or enhances their reputations and leads to increased confidence on their part and on the part of others, thus leading to increased probability of success on other ideas and actions. In essence, a snowball effect creates momentum, and they and their unit are able to keep rolling on accomplishing various goals and establishing themselves as outstanding performers.

From time to time in those early months, there may be setbacks and stumbles, but that is to be expected and natural, for indeed you can't hit a home run or even get a hit every time at bat. One can look at most individuals' first year as being divided into the first few months when they become acclimated to the organization, thereafter their proposing and implementing various ideas and changes, and then fine-tuning them to achieve maximum effectiveness and efficiency. Once they have been in charge of the unit for a year or two, there will be a second round or wave of ideas, changes, and modifications.

In the first few months and then for a year, or two, or three, these individuals, whether they are a president, vice president, division head, or even a small unit head, have established themselves and earned some kind of reputation, either good or bad. Assuming it is a good-to-great reputation, the real issue is how well does he or she wear?

There are many who can look good, accomplish significant results, and get along well with supervisors, peers, and subordinates for the short run while their initial enthusiasm is high and the honeymoon period is in effect. But once the newness of the responsibilities wears off and one is no longer the new supervisor or star, the person's ideas, drive, attention to detail, or human relations skills may falter. Alternatively, the good ideas may just not work, or they may falter because of forces either within the individual's control or beyond it. Or, the bright new ways that a new person brings may have been exhausted and he or she is not able to maintain the pace of innovation and change. Instead of operating in a creative mode, with a mind-set for new approaches, he or she may have to operate in a maintenance mode, as much as possible keeping things on an even keel. Furthermore, the organization or unit may face difficult times due to external or internal factors so that a new person is constrained in what can be done, advancement and significant increases in compensation and responsibilities are blocked, changes occur in the organization so that stress increases, and there are disagreements in regard to policies, practices, and style, culminating in personal attacks.

The question then for all involved is how is the individual able to face the various vicissitudes of organizational life, the day-to-day responsibilities, the humdrum, the crises, and the opportunities? Over a period of years, do the person's work habits, attitudes, performance, style, dedication, personality and human relations skills continue or improve? In comparison with those first months, or first year or two, is there steady growth or is there a significant decline? In essence, no matter how well the person started, the key to how well he or she will succeed in the organization over time is how comfortable we feel with the person once we have time to see him or her day in and day out in a wide variety of situations. Many have faltered and not gone further in an organization, or they have left, because, in effect, they wear thin. Those who wear consistently well are those who are most likely to succeed.

32

YOU CAN'T GO HOME AGAIN

———————— ✕ ————————

At times, when things are not going right or have not gone right for a long time in your present position, or your expectations have not been met and appear unreachable, you look back with nostalgia to your former position, or to former responsibilities in the company, or to your previous employer. You begin to dwell on how happy you were then, to kick yourself for having made a change, or for reaching beyond your grasp. You may have dreams about returning to your old spot or at least to your old division or company, and you may even take steps to reestablish contact and return.

This scene may occur at any time in your career. Those going through a mid-career crisis or who have failed to get the hoped-for promotion or big bonus are particularly vulnerable to nostalgic idealization of the past. Your past association or the other opportunities you gave up when you took this one may have been all that you now think they were. It is probable, however, that time and your present concerns have blocked out from your memory the reasons that made you want to leave your former position or decide not to take certain opportunities. In any event, it is unlikely that if you really pursued it, your previous employer would want you back—times may have changed, your replacement may be better than you, and so on. And if you did go back, assuming you have been away for some time, you would probably find that reality was far different than you imagined.

The important thing is that neither figuratively nor literally can one go back home again. If you understand that, you can deal more effectively with past accomplishments and associations as you compare them with what seems to be a less favorable present and future, and you can concentrate on the here and now rather than the there and then.

You can't recapture the past and ride its coattails to the future. And you can't afford to dwell too much on former glories (whether absolutely accurate or embellished by desire and time). By dwelling on a puffed-up or idealized past or even a realistic past, you tend to negate possibilities now and in the future. You build barriers to working through your present problems, even if working through involves changing positions or companies. You may indeed have made an error in your choice of new position, but the healthy way of dealing with it is not dwelling on the past and saying, Why did I leave?

The healthy and productive way is to see what you can do realistically about the situation and develop a plan of attack. The productive way of dealing with the past, if you're comparing it very favorably with the present, is to search for things that were wrong with your former life or position so that at least you bring some perspective to the picture. Even if there was little wrong, you can review what made you make the change, either the bad aspects in the former role or the anticipated good ones in the new role. You may find that some of the elements of enjoyment and challenge are still there, but you have let them slip by.

Beyond comparisons, you can learn from your old position those aspects that bring you satisfaction and dissatisfaction and can then try to build on these in your present position and life, or you can at least augment your learning about them through your present experience as you search for new positions and lifestyles.

It may be difficult and painful to recognize that you're no longer part of that old group or company, just as there are pangs of nostalgia when you get together with your old crowd at the 25th high school or college reunion. But we can take those memories, experiences, skills, and attitudes built and developed in former associations and use them to improve our outlook on life today and on our hope for tomorrow. The old "home" is a nice place to visit, but since it is an old you, you can't live there anymore. You have grown beyond it, but you can use the knowledge and strength you have gained to make your present and future "homes"—the present and future you—better.

33

BEWARE OF THE HIGH
ACHIEVER'S DISEASE

You may have the executive's equivalent of blue-collar blues and white-collar woes. Just as those on the assembly line or in clerical and administrative positions burn out, top out, and face problems of job dissatisfaction, there is also a very debilitating and costly disease to individuals and companies: Manager's Malaise—Boredom and Blahs.

To identify whether you have or may get the disease, take the following quiz. Answers should be recorded: (a) Very Frequently or Always; (b) Frequently; (c) Fairly Often; (d) Sometimes; (e) Rarely; (f) Very Rarely or Never.

1. Do you have a sense of being bored with assignments?
2. As you look to the schedule for the next work day, week, or month, do you feel bored, unexcited, or unstimulated by what's ahead?
3. Do you suffer from headaches, stomach distress, rashes, or other ailments that occur frequently and tend to linger?
4. Have you been feeling sick and/or taking more time off for illness?
5. Are you overeating (or undereating), smoking more, or drinking more?
6. Do you regard lunch as the best part of your day?
7. Do you look at the time frequently to see how close it is to quitting time?
8. Is it harder to get out of bed in the morning than it used to be?
9. Does the Thank God It's Friday feeling occur?

10. Do you have a Thank God It's Thursday or Thank God It's Wednesday and the week will soon be over feeling?

11. Is it hard for you to go to work on Mondays?

12. Do you get headaches or feel depressed or irritable on Sundays?

13. Do you have fight with people on and off the job?

14. Are you lethargic when you are off from work?

15. Are you hyperactive when you are off from work?

16. Are you lethargic when at work?

17. Are you hyperactive when at work?

18. Do you feel depressed at work for more than an hour or two or, at most, a day or two?

19. Do you feel depressed at home for more than an hour or two or, at most, a day or two?

20. Do you go from extreme highs to extreme lows in terms of your feelings about work or your life in general?

21. Do you have very little or nothing to say about your job?

22. Do you find that you're spending more time on a job but accomplishing the same or less than you used to?

23. Although your job responsibilities are the same as in the past, are you more likely to evaluate your performance in terms of creating a good atmosphere and good human relations than in striving for specific, concrete job achievement?

24. Are you spending less time at work (leaving early, coming in late, longer lunch hours, more frequent coffee breaks, concentrating on non-job-related activities)?

25. Do you hate to come back from a vacation, or do you keep looking forward to vacations and count the days—more so than in the past?

26. Do you have a feeling of *not* wanting to accomplish anything important in the next week, month, six months, or year?

27. As you look back over your work effort over the last week, month, or three months, do you have a sense that what you did wasn't particularly important, worthwhile, challenging, or stimulating?

28. Do you feel that a great percentage of the things you do is trivial and could be done by someone two or three levels beneath you?

29. As you look closely at what you do, does it seem as if a lot of it is filling up the time—doing busy work, paying too much attention to detail, being too finicky, sending things back to get them perfect, scheduling unnecessary meetings, or prolonging conversation or meetings unnecessarily?

30. Do you measure the success of a day, week, or month by the criterion that nothing went wrong or you kept the lid on, rather than what went right?

Score yourself as follows. For each question you answered:

Very Frequently or Always: Score 5 points
Frequently: Score 4 points
Fairly Often: Score 3 points
Sometimes: Score 2 points
Rarely: Score 1 point
Very Rarely or Never: Score 0

Total the score. If you have 100 or more, you have a very severe case of Manager's Malaise; unless immediate action is taken, the disease can be fatal for your job, career, or psychological health. A score of 75-90 indicates that you have a severe case; job, career, and family life are significantly threatened and very quick action is necessary or you will quickly reach extremis. A score of 50-74 means there's a case of Manager's Malaise; job, career, and family life are threatened and action is necessary to prevent the disease from getting worse. With a score of 25-49, you may be on the verge of getting the disease; plan carefully how to prevent becoming ill and beware of the early signs of exposure to the disease. Under 25—you're OK!

MANAGER'S MALAISE—WHAT IS IT?

This malaise is captured in many of the 30 questions raised earlier. It is a feeling of not being as productive as you could be. It is a feeling of not being sufficiently challenged, stimulated, or excited by the job now and as you look down the road; a feeling that present and future problems and opportunities are not new or taxing or that they are trivial, humdrum, or boring; a belief that your brain, energy, creativity, talent, and potential are not being tapped as fully and as frequently as possible. You feel that future prospects are relatively bleak, that what is done by you, your superiors, and your organization doesn't matter very much and isn't done with any real distinction or style. You have the feeling that the organization and the individuals in it are really second rate and will remain that way, that you are losing your drive, ambition, and dreams of high achievement and contribution, that you are becoming a second rater yourself—albeit a first-rate second rater!

CAUSES OF MANAGER'S MALAISE

Successful managers tend to be motivated by and receive a high degree of job satisfaction from a variety of factors. These include interesting responsibilities, range of responsibilities, challenge, stimulation, impact on the organization, recognition, compensation, status, relationship with superiors and others, ability to innovate, being your own boss or having your own time, freedom to act, the pace of work, quality of the organization and its people, and future possibilities for and in the organization.

In addition, there is the concern for continued learning and growth on the job, a sense of climbing the learning and growth curve. Talented people remain jazzed up, motivated, zestful, and highly creative and productive when they feel that what they're doing today or this year is significantly better and more challenging than what they did last year. High achievers want to acquire, improve on, and demonstrate abilities, skills, and knowledge that they didn't have before or had to a substantially lesser degree. They want to feel they've advanced from one point on the curve to a higher point in terms of knowledge and performance. Executives invest so much of their egos in their jobs that when they find themselves running in place rather than climbing higher or sprinting, they get down on themselves. If high achievers have hit a plateau during their climb, they are likely to be bored and disinterested.

There are other causes. The individual can be going through the midlife crisis when one begins to question one's life, career, goals, job, and marital relationship. In effect, the person asks, What I am going to do with the rest of my life when today is the first day of the rest of my life; what are my values and goals; what do I want to do on the job and off; in what organizational setting and with whom?

Another frequent cause of malaise is the environment found on the job or in the organization. This may take the form of general and industrywide economic stagnation or recession and, thus, less opportunities for change, growth, innovation, mergers, and acquisitions; increased foreign and domestic competition; smaller profits resulting in decreased (or no) compensation increases for the individual and the staff; high turnover in the company; greater responsibilities because of staff cuts; more regulations and red tape; generally greater pressures on the job; more competition among units for increasingly scarce resources; concern about job security or about remaining in the same geographic area or division in the company; concern about mergers or acquisitions that might affect one's job or future; change in the atmosphere in the organization because of any or all of the above so that work is less fun and more tension-filled, while more backbiting prevails.

At times, simply as a combination of pressures in climbing the learning and growth curve or the executive ladder, or in dealing with years of stress or with the same problems, you may be burned out. You can also be topped out in that you have reached your earnings or responsibility and position peak due to your own limitations and/or conditions in the company or industry that are beyond your influence or control. Given the economy or your present compensation, you may not be able to get as good a job in the same industry or in any industry.

POSSIBLE REMEDIES

For each individual and company, the remedy or combination of remedies may be different. In many cases, the individual should first have a thorough physical checkup as some physical or physiological problem may be the major or contributing cause of malaise. Barring that, in some cases it might be best for the company and the individual if the individual changed his or her job or career. However, before taking such a major step, there are some actions that are worth attempting. Both the company and the individual must be committed to understanding the potential seriousness of the situation and the necessity for careful planning and action to cure the symptoms, manifestations, and underlying causes of the disease. On the part of the company, there must be greater concern for people within the organization, and there must be understanding of the effect the corporation culture, climate, and style has on individuals. The company must learn how conditions can be improved to meet the needs of people while meeting corporate goals. People needs should be a major corporate goal.

SPECIFIC ACTIONS TO OVERCOME MANAGER'S MALAISE

1. Change and vary breadth, depth, and type of assignments and expand scope of responsibilities, including special project assignments.

2. Get new knowledge, acquired through education, training, seminars, and conferences.

3. Expose yourself to public and community activities and speaking and writing opportunities, including part-time and full-time public or community service assignments.

4. Have opportunities to serve and lead inter- and intradepartmental committees or task forces, interorganization and industrywide activities, committees, and task forces.

5. Obtain opportunities for short- or long-term travel or relocation.

6. Generate new interests in hobbies and recreational activities; broaden your intellectual and cultural knowledge and interests.

7. Increase opportunities for regular exercise.

8. Improve relationships with your family and friends; show more concern about them and their interests.

9. Talk about your frustrations and malaise with your spouse, trusted friends, or perhaps your supervisor or someone else in the company (if this does not carry a significant risk of hurting your career). It may be necessary to seek professional counseling.

10. Expose yourself in depth to some hands-on experience in the newest techniques and technology in the fields of your primary responsibilities and interests, in allied or related fields, or in potential areas of responsibility. This can range from product development, to human relations, to operations research, computer technology, and so on.

11. Set ambitious and tough personal and professional goals for yourself and your unit and its staff and strive to attain them. Include a concern for creativity and innovation, planning, implementation, control, communication, evaluation, and development of staff.

12. Help to set ambitious and tough objectives for the organization and work with others to achieve them.

13. Change or modify your work habits and work schedule. Intersperse interesting topics, meetings, and problems each day or week with more humdrum ones so as to break up your day. Learn to pace yourself so as to focus on important items and to treat trivialities lightly.

14. Practice time management and stress management techniques. Recognize that the goal of time management is to make time available for important efforts.

15. Occasionally, use lunchtime to relax and recharge yourself by focusing on nonbusiness topics and persons rather than on the usual work-related lunch.

The organization that fails to deal with the problems and possibilities of individuals falling prey to or having Manager's Malaise is failing to fully utilize the effectiveness and contribution of its most precious resource—the talented individual. That individual, in turn, who does not look objectively at being a potential or actual victim of Manager's Malaise—what is causing it and what can be done

MOTIVATION AND LEADERSHIP

about it—may well end up performing well below potential, below previous performance and par, and may be caught feeling trapped and unfulfilled.

34

MOTIVATION AND LEADERSHIP

———— ✕ ————

Much has been written about the topics of motivation and leadership. Those interested in these subjects can soon be overwhelmed by concepts such as Theory X–Theory Y; satisfiers–dissatisfiers; hierarchy of needs; Systems 1–4; job enrichment; leadership contingency model; managerial grid, and so on. I offer a personal view about this important matter based on writings in the field and my own experience.

In regard to leadership, you should recognize that the success of your style of leadership will depend on factors within yourself (your personality, intelligence, drive, skills, and so forth) and within your subordinates, peers, and superiors; the environment, history, and traditions within the unit and the organization; and internal and external factors affecting the particular situation and group.

You lead by more than charisma or knowledge alone. You have to have an understanding of what motivates most people, recognizing that each person is quite different and what may motivate him or her, or be an appropriate leadership style at one point in time, may not be effective some months or years later. These are basic concerns that most employees, at all levels, have:

1. Is the work interesting and satisfying?
2. Does the organization provide the necessary resources and a good working environment?

chtame.

3. Is sufficient responsibility, authority, and information provided to accomplish the goals set?

4. Is the compensation system (including amounts paid) fair?

5. Is there an opportunity to develop special skills and abilities, to grow, learn, be recognized, and rewarded?

6. Is there security on the job—emotional and psychological as well as security of employment?

7. Can one get a sense of accomplishment, involvement, consultation, and control to some degree over one's fate?

You will have to use different approaches on different individuals and situations. In general, I have found it effective to focus on:

• Acting with integrity and decency toward others.

• Demonstrating a genuine concern about what is happening to others on the job—their challenges, frustration, aspirations, recognition, and reward.

• Understanding the effect that poor working conditions, atmosphere, and supervision can have on people's work efforts and on their physical, psychological and emotional life, on their sense of self-worth and on their families.

• Setting an example of high standards of performance, dedication, integrity, and loyalty, and expecting the same from others.

• Providing adequate psychic income as well as monetary income and demonstrating concern for Manager's Malaise (see Chapter 33).

In regard to motivation, I have indicated elsewhere in the book the importance of providing psychic income to the individual and creating an organizational culture and environment that brings out the best in people and provides the basis for increasing job satisfaction. However, we must recognize that some of the traditional thinking about motivation is outmoded. For example, I would argue that the idea that people don't matter quite as much in the highly automated workplace is wrong. As we introduce more technology into the workplace, people will have more individual control over the effort they expend on the job, and thus, their satisfaction is even more important than in the past. Another mistaken idea is that increased job satisfaction necessarily leads to increased productivity. People may be happier because of office parties and workplace layout, but their productivity will probably not increase unless morale-raising efforts are tied to motivation in regard to productivity. Many of us also assume that the work ethic has declined. I suggest that many people work to develop themselves as people—to learn, to grow—in addition to the basic idea of working to improve their standards of living.

If you want to motivate effectively, I suggest that compensation, both monetary and psychic, must be tied to the performance of the individual and group. Although making the job more agreeable is important, what will be more effective as a motivational force is pay tied to performance and opportunities for increased responsibility and advancement. If you want to increase productivity, you must insist on high standards of performance, quality, and service. There must be a sense that individuals at all levels are important as human beings and as productive members of the organization and are to be treated with dignity.

Finally, I turn to the issue of monetary compensation since elsewhere I have discussed nonmonetary compensation. A paycheck has four different meanings to an individual. The paycheck is compensation for the individual giving his or her effort and time. It indicates the individual's market value. The paycheck can be seen as a reward and incentive. It can also be viewed as an investment in the person in order to develop the person and to meet the organization's future needs.

In deciding on the size of the paycheck, the organization might choose different evaluation criteria such as contribution to profitability, effectiveness, efficiency, service, and quantity and quality of work. Ideally, these evaluations would fit within a job evaluation system that ranks positions by difficulty and responsibility. Such a system would also set salary ranges based on survey data of salaries paid for comparable positions. In establishing ranges, the organization should be concerned with internal and external equity.

In effect, monetary compensation can fulfill its four functions, or meanings, and in so doing indicate to the employee management's assessment of present performance and potential for the future.

Motivation and leadership issues are of such great significance that they are well worth considerable concern and discussion within all organizations. The effective and sensitive implementation of a motivational and leadership approach and style are critical factors in the success of individuals as leaders and managers and in the success of any organization.

35

TO THINE OWN SELF . . .

There are situations, people, issues—indeed, organizations—in which, in order to succeed or even survive, you will have to be very tough. You might have to use a style that goes beyond the analogy of a gloved fist to an ungloved fist; that goes, in fact, to an analogy of the bare fist to brass knuckles. If you are uncomfortable in dealing with such circumstances in this manner, it would be best for you to find another position or organization. (Of course, it may depend on how often you have to use the fist and brass knuckles.) It appears in some organizations that the toughest and meanest are the ones who get the most rewards. You have to decide how tough and mean you are or want to be, whether this is the climate in which you want to work, and what are the costs or benefits of the rewards and recognition.

It is also true that in other organizations or at particular times in any organization the person who is regarded as an individual with integrity, high standards of personal and professional conduct, as well as outstanding managerial ability gets the promotion and the power. In essence, there is no guarantee that good guys will finish first, second, or last. It may well depend on conditions over which an individual and the organization may have little control.

However others regard you, you have to be honest with yourself. You know when you have stabbed someone in the back, manipulated data and people, taken unfair advantage of a situation, mistake, or weakness. At times, you may justify the action as being distasteful but necessary for the good of the unit or company or for your own career. Other times, you may recognize the Machiavellian approach you have used, but justify it by the argument "the end justifies the means." Whatever the reason or rationale for your action, at least understand what you have done, and why, and the effect it may have on your reputation. Furthermore, understand that once you get into a pattern of dirty tricks and actions that are morally and professionally on the borderline or worse, you will have difficulty reversing yourself, and you will tend to stonewall, cover up, and cross the borderline faster and deeper each time. Although you may comfort your conscience by saying, *Once I get to the top, I'll play by the rules,* it is unlikely you will be able to cleanse yourself. You may also have set in motion an organizational climate that stresses underhanded actions and people who are lying in wait for revenge.

It is important to have a conscience, to follow it, to have a sense of what's right and wrong. In the end, you will face the judgment of your colleagues, but, most of all, you will have to look at yourself in the mirror and decide whether you are where you are through honest means or through deceit and dishonesty. Decency and integrity may not result in your being at the top, but, at least, for people of conscience, this will ensure that you can look yourself in the eye and not be ashamed.

36

I SHOULD HAVE SPENT MORE TIME AT THE OFFICE

A popular cliché in conversation and psychotherapy is that on a deathbed no one ever says, "I wish I had spent more time at the office." The point, apparently universally accepted, is that real meaning, pleasure, and fulfillment in life are derived from relationships with loved ones, family, and friends and from various interests having very little or nothing to do with one's job or career.

The cliché implies that on your deathbed you will regret that first, you did not spend more time and energy developing, strengthening, and nurturing these relationships and interests and, second, that you did not spend more time developing yourself both as an individual and as a member of a family or community. You will regret you did not have more fun and take time to smell the roses.

The attitude expressed is important. It addresses the relevant issue that there is much more to life and to an individual than what he or she does for a living. Over the past two decades, Americans have rebelled against the Calvinist work ethic, Type A personalities, workaholics, the "disloyalty" shown by organizations in their massive layoffs and benefit-cutting. We have turned toward understanding, developing, and pleasing our outer and inner selves.

But in our rebellion, we may have gone too far. We may have lost that striving to be excellent and that impetus to do more by stretching ourselves. We may not be putting in the time, energy, and effort to strive to be very good at what we do in our jobs and careers. Adequacy or better-than-average suffices for many because seeking to be more requires the kind of dedication to the job and the organization that cuts into the time and energy available for nonwork activities.

Individuals need a balance of work, relationships, and interests and involvements. But work has been receiving, at most, a one-third share. If we are to be the best we can at work—with the impact this would bring to our organizations, industries, communities and nation—more of us should be concerned that the tilt away from work has gone too far.

Dedication is a two-way street. Organizations must demonstrate a new or renewed dedication to employees. An enterprise worthy of an individual's commitment and dedication pays attention to such quality-of-worklife issues as breaking down hierarchies, emphasis on teamwork and meaningful work, opportunities to develop employee potential and interests, appropriate monetary and psychic compensation, and concern for corporate culture.

What is needed is the creation of a workplace atmosphere in which employees give their fullest energies, talents, and enthusiasm toward making each workday productive, effective, and efficient. They don't hold back their creativity, intelligence, and energy for non-work pursuits. Excelling at meaningful work can equal the success in other aspects of life. We need to believe that what we do and how we do it is important to the organization and to ourselves. Our goals should be that both we and our employer are as good as we can be. There is meaningful work to be accomplished, whether from 9-to-5 or, dare we say, 9-to-6 and more. We "owe" our organizations, colleagues, customers, supervisors, and direct reports, and they "owe" us.

We might lead more meaningful lives professionally and personally if we were to consider adopting the deathbed cliché, "I wish I had spent more time at the office." Work at the office is not unworthy of great dedication; our careers require full measures of devotion.

37

THE TITLE TRAP

He loves his title but hates his job. She loves her position but is bored with her responsibilities. He likes his title, power, and salary; he just can't stand what he does.

Sound familiar? Why is it that people—from newly minted MBAs to CEOs—so often feel dissatisfied or discontent with their jobs? While they may find that the compensation, perks, and prestige of the job are considerable and comforting, many of the actual day-to-day responsibilities can be less than satisfying.

In any organization, a certain amount of "trivia" is involved in every job. High-ranking executives may wonder why they have to deal with insignificant matters they feel could be handled one, two, or three levels below them. At the same time, entry-level professionals may wonder, given their usual day-to-day routine, why they needed a graduate degree—or even a college degree—at all.

As individuals climb the ladder of success, their challenge is to get a balance of stimulating activities, humdrum duties, and outright trivia. Hopefully, you can keep the humdrum and trivial duties as negligible as possible. But if an executive has been doing the same director/vice president job for a long period in the same division, company, or even industry, and if the company is either standing still or in decline (no new major products, services, expansion, mergers and acquisitions, or other opportunities to face), what in the past was exciting may now be routine. And what once was merely routine, now may seem even worse.

GOLDEN HANDCUFFS

Given all this, a high-level employee may feel trapped by the "good life" that has been achieved as a result of a title, especially if the satisfaction that goes along with it is negligible. So, what happens next? If the employee reaches the point of not being able to put up with the frustration or the friction of the job, it may be very difficult—for psychological reasons as well as marketability—to take on a more meaningful and potentially more satisfying job with another organization, but with a less prestigious title (and the compensation and perks that go with it).

The individual also may find the job search difficult if he or she is currently "overtitled." Some companies provide prestigious titles in lieu of greater compensation. Thus, trapped by title, the executive may decide (voluntarily or involuntarily) to accept a lower title and/or a lower salary outside the company. Accepting a lower title often can be harder than accepting a pay cut, unless it comes with a rational explanation—such as a move to a more prestigious organization.

What does this mean for those who feel that they could not obtain a comparable or higher title in another organization? What does it mean for those who don't want to give up the security of their present positions even though they are unhappy with the content of the job?

The answer to this dilemma comes from understanding one's own psychological makeup. How important are financial, prestige, power, and status compensation—to you and to those who are important to you—and how much satisfaction do you get in job content? How much of a risk-taker are you? What are your immediate, short- and long-range financial obligations? What prestige and status opportunities does the new job offer?

Depending on one's age, stage of career, marketability, and the other previously cited factors, the executive may decide that the title is not worth the frustration, anguish, unhappiness, and lack of fulfillment and accomplishment. He or she might then decide that a job title change, even a downward shift, is necessary to achieve personal satisfaction. And if things break right, the executive might achieve an equivalent or a higher title but in a job that provides significant satisfaction in content and activities.

If, for one reason or another, the executive decides to stay put (and before making a job change, these actions should be considered first), he or she can take action to feel and think better about the job. The following are several suggestions:

- Try to expand the breadth and depth of those things that are most stimulating.
- Seek temporary assignments or position rotation assignments, perhaps leading to interesting more long-term assignments.
- Tackle new and different issues—both short- and long-term.
- Delegate or relinquish as much of the humdrum or trivia as possible.
- Seek to serve on committees, task forces, or special projects that expand your knowledge, skills, interests, and your resumé.
- Get involved as the organization's representative in professional, industry, and community affairs.

A health checkup and longer or more frequent vacations may also be in order (often a high achiever may be physically or emotionally exhausted). Talking about frustrations, goals, midcareer or even peak-career crises with friends or counselors can also help. Explore new hobbies, community service, and those things you have never done before or stopped doing years ago. This change of pace or enthusiasm that adds zest to nonbusiness hours may carry over to new feelings and approaches toward work.

For some, the title trap can be very real. The strength of the trap, and how deeply it affects your life and career, will depend on your capacity to deal with the frustrations at hand and your willingness to take the risks and actions necessary to break or at least stretch the bars that trap you.

38

THE TEN COMMANDMENTS
OF MANAGEMENT

The great surge of books about management and the outstanding popular success several have achieved make it clear that improvement of one's self and one's organization, as well as the individual's and organization's chances for success, are of increasing concern to many individuals.

The successful manager applies both the art and the science of management. The science of management consists of the various theories, concepts, practices, techniques, processes, and technology that can be applied (modified as necessary) to management issues, situations, and problems. The art of management involves leadership, sensitivity, empathy, creativity—a concern for the organization environment and culture. The successful manager combines some of the skills, approaches, and insights of the artist, salesperson, inventor, dreamer, spokesperson, entrepreneur, planner, crisis handler, counselor, preacher, warrior, diplomat, operator, negotiator, leader, and philosopher. The manager is a boss, colleague, peer, subordinate, teacher, student, mentor, role model, and disciple.

These complexities make it almost impossible to summarize briefly the essence of outstanding management. However, if I were allowed only three to five minutes to talk about how to achieve success in management, I would offer the Biblical Ten Commandments as adapted to management.

The *Ten Commandments of Management* are presented as a guide to personal success. The Biblical Commandments address an individual's relationship to God and to other individuals; the following Management Ten Commandments address an individual's relationship to the organization and to other individuals:

I   Large short- and long-term profit and return on investment are the lord thy god of management who led thee out of the land of mediocrity, bankruptcy, and dissolution, *out* of the house of despair and defeat.

II   Remember the paramount pillars of outstanding management—the necessity for thorough planning; sound judgment and decision making; careful, creative implementation and monitoring of decisions and operations; and a concern for people and results, based on first-rate management skills and management style. These skills involve planning, organizing, staffing, deciding, budgeting, innovating, communicating, representing, controlling, directing, and motivating. Another approach to managerial skills is offered by Herbert Mintzberg who lists as skills: developing peer relationships carrying out negotiations, motivating subordinates, resolving conflicts, establishing information networks, and subsequently disseminating information-making decisions in conditions of extreme ambiguity, and allocating resources. Management style depends on the attributes and characteristics of the individual, his or her subordinates, peers and superiors, and of the organization at a particular time. The organization's culture and climate will also be important in determining an appropriate style. Style can range from authoritarian to democratic, participative to dictatorial, production oriented to people oriented, widely open to tightly shut.

III   Thou shalt not commit perjury, disloyalty, or bring dishonor to thy colleagues, or organization or profession.

IV   Honor and respect thy mentors, superiors, peers, subordinates, and colleagues so that thy days may be long with the organization and in the executive ranks of management and so that thou shalt be respected as a loyal individual.

V   Thou shalt not covet thy colleague's or competitor's title, salary, organization, office, staff, or resources, but rather learn from them and the situation so that you can progress and prevail in the struggle to climb higher faster.

VI   Thou shalt not bear false witness against those within or outside the organization nor slander, defame, misrepresent—personal, professional, and organizational integrity shall be paramount.

VII   Thou shalt not steal, bribe, or be bribed; accept various types of gratuities that are given in anticipation of favors now or in the future; falsify expense accounts, results or facts or conceal figures or safety or performance tests.

VIII   Thou shalt not murder new ideas, innovative or unusual approaches, departures from or questioning of the status quo, but instead shall encourage a questioning attitude, creativity, risk-taking, and innovation.

IX   Thou shalt not forsake your sense of humanity and sensitivity and concern for others, your organization, community, and nation. Whatever your level of success in the organization, you should be able to look yourself in the mirror in regard to your primary role as a human being.

X   Thou shalt not cease in striving for excellence for yourself, your colleagues, and your organization in all aspects of the art and science of management.

The Commandments have to be interpreted and applied narrowly or broadly depending on the situation, the organization, and the individuals involved. They offer guidance and beacons in facing the complexities and challenges, the opportunities and satisfactions of modern-day management.

39

RIGHTSIZE—DOWNSIZE IF NECESSARY, BUT REMEMBER THE VICTIMS AND SURVIVORS

Downsizing organizations, making them lean, more efficient, tougher, is the name of the game currently and is likely to continue over the next decade. Rightsizing is the newer name for the process and has a better ring to it—we're getting it right! It is indeed true that many organizations have added new functions and activities or expanded others, thereby adding costs for staff, space, equipment, and various overhead and other cost areas that can be cut back during tough, competitive times. And over time organizations have added similar costs in their core functions. These also need "rightsizing" if such organizations are to remain financially sound and competitive against those who have already bitten the bullet and rightsized, as well as against new organizations. Many of the new companies that have sprung up are built on a very lean, tough, model with state-of-the-art technology and systems in production, distribution, marketing, communications, information, finance, and so on. So, whether the word applied is rightsizing, downsizing, reengineering, reconfiguring, value engineering, or benchmarking, the end result is fewer staff.

In planning for rightsizing, it is important to have regard for the victims. Many are long service employees who have given much of their working careers to the organization and industry, have tried hard, and through no or little fault of their own, will now bear the brunt of what may indeed be the right thing for the organization and for those who will remain employed. Those to be let go may have been capable of and eager for retraining but the company may not have had the money, time, or foresight to retrain and retool their people just as they needed to retool their equipment, systems, and processes. Now, many in their 40s, 50s, and 60s face the difficulty of finding new jobs and perhaps new careers since the industry they are in, as a whole, might have been downsized or perhaps even destroyed. And they face the formidable challenge at a time when because of downsizing in all areas, the competition for jobs is very great.

It is in the organization's best interest, not just because it is the "right thing to do," to deal as fairly as possible with those who will have to leave. The way they are treated sends a signal to those who remain as to whether there is human sensitivity to the issue at hand and not just a financial sensitivity. Consideration should be given to being as generous and concerned as possible in regard to notice given, severance package, continuation of benefits, assistance in planning, preparing, and searching for new jobs and careers, opportunities for retraining.

Having taken the difficult steps of letting people go, of eliminating functions, activities, departments, of reconfiguring and merging those that remain, too often, organizations don't pay enough attention to those who survived and remain employed.

Many survivors will worry about whether they still will have a job in three or six months or for the next year or two. The organization has to debate whether to do its cutting in one fell swoop or in stages or waves. Aside from concern and stress about their job security, very often employees experience even more stress because of the work they now are asked to perform. Rightsizing often eliminates functions and activities, institutes better systems and procedures and substitutes modern technology for old technology (or no technology) and for people. If done correctly, this process enables a company to do the same or perhaps even more with fewer people. Often, however, the ideal does not occur and those who remain are expected to do a lot more than they did before with resources (equipment, systems, space, funds, and staff) not adequate for the demands on them. A staff of 10, with some newer computer technology may be asked to achieve what a staff of 15 or 20 or 25 achieved before. The better equipment may just not be able to make up the gap and even better supervision, compensation, motivation, and procedures may still not make up for very large reductions.

The wise organization, in embarking on the rightsizing path, will spend considerable time planning, anticipating, and involving. They will plan very carefully what the goals and objectives will be and who will do what. They will anticipate what could go wrong, and better yet, what is necessary to prevent things from going wrong. And, very important, they will involve those who will survive in the planning and anticipating. Aside from real involvement, the top executives need to be concerned about reassuring the survivors about their future in the organization and that they will not be exploited. They will be given the resources needed and an organization and communication structure, policies, and procedures that promote effectiveness and efficiency; the time to adjust; the recognition of the difficulty of what lies ahead; employee assistance programs to help them deal with the stress and the readjustment necessary; and, if finances permit, monetary as well as other recognition of what is expected of them. Certainly, there should be financial and other recognition when they achieve objectives.

There should be recognition, also, that rightsizing sometimes results in what has been referred to as "corporate anorexia." The corporation in seeking to reduce costs and staff (an American Management Association study indicated that generally profits increased at big companies that downsized from 1989 to 1994, but worker productivity did not increase appreciably and morale declined sharply), often reduces its ability to grow and innovate. Leanness can become anorexia with great harm to the organization, short- and long-term, as well as to employees in the strain placed on them.

A rightsized organization needs the skills, loyalty, and dedication of its employees, at all levels, even more than previously. But loyalty and dedication will need to be earned by the organization and its top executives. In a sense, the organization has been "destroyed" by breaking what may have seemed to be a contract between employees at all levels and the employer: "If I work hard and do my job, I'll have a job and opportunities for job advancement and satisfaction." The "contract" may have had to be broken by forces well beyond the employee's control but now as more is demanded and expected of those who remain, the wise employer will seek to build a strong foundation, a new contract with employees.

40

LEADERSHIP NOW AND IN THE NEXT DECADE—VISION, PASSION, KNOWLEDGE, AND KNOW-HOW

I have spent more than 30 years in managerial positions, read thousands of resumés, interviewed hundreds of applicants for executive positions and, most important, observed and worked with hundreds of executives on the job. These experiences have led me to believe that what one is trying to identify in reading resumés, interviewing or evaluating performance, and working with executives is the quality of strong leadership or the potential for strong leadership. In my view, the truly successful leader demonstrates very high levels of accomplishment in four areas—vision, passion, knowledge, and know-how.

A leader needs to have a vision (hopefully, a creative, successful vision) of what he or she wants his or her unit, department, division, company to accomplish in the short and long term. What are the overarching goals and objectives that stretch the organization today and position it to more than hold its own tomorrow and in the long-term future, to be a significant player in its industry, in the region, in the economy? Without a strong vision, which makes all concerned run hard, the leader is not a leader but merely a manager of the status quo. Organizations without vision are doomed to fall behind in the race for success and probably will fall out of the race to be overtaken, overcome, acquired by, or forced out of business by those with vision.

In addition to a vision, the leader needs the passion to execute the vision. He or she has to get others to buy into the vision, to adopt it as a shared vision, and in turn, to be passionate about bringing about a shared vision and its accomplishment in their own efforts and in the efforts of others. The passion can be exhibited quietly or in a more outgoing manner, in a charismatic or noncharismatic way, depending on the personality and style of the leader. But however the style and tone of communication, there is the sense of deep and abiding and long-lasting concern and commitment, that this is a vision worth fighting and working very hard for; worth sacrificing for; worth, indeed, blood, sweat, and tears.

These two abilities and characteristics are the basic foundation—without them, one can at most fight a holding action. But to succeed, the highly successful leader must have the knowledge of the issues, opportunities, problems, the external and internal factors impacting on the organization and industry, on the vision. He or she need not be an outstanding expert in each aspect of the knowledge necessary for success, for the leader can hire or find staff or consultants with truly expert knowledge. But the leader does need to know when and what he or she doesn't know, and to be able to understand or learn to understand the issues and facts in sufficient detail to make informed judgments and to make choices among differing views.

Even if the leader has the "right" vision, degrees of passion, and knowledge of the issue, he or she needs to have "know-how"—the ability to get things done, to gain acceptance of the vision, passion, and knowledge—to deliver on the promise of the vision. Knowledge isn't necessarily know-how, nor is vision and passion. History is replete with examples in every sector of the economy and in government of those with vision, passion, and strong intellect and knowledge who through weakness or gaps in know-how could not translate ideas into action. Thus, an understanding of the culture of the organization, of how to bring about the acceptance of change, of the psychological aspects of management, knowing how policies, practices, processes work or don't work, questions of style and personality, of organizational and planning skills, of a sense of timing, of having a "political sense," of communication skills, of people skills, all of these and more get to the critical issue of know-how.

The four factors/skills/abilities—vision, passion, knowledge, know-how—and the degree to which the individual has each of these will determine the level of success and indeed the historic contribution the individual can make to the organization.

41

To Achieve Early Positive Notice at a New Position or Assignment— Look for Small Quick Victories

When you are new to a position, assignment, or company, you need to establish in the eyes of others, as well as for yourself, that you are able to contribute, make a difference, be, in fact, a "player." After having done that, you will, depending on your ambition, opportunities, and skills, seek to become a "major player." But before advancing to a higher level of influence and contribution, you must establish yourself in your new assignment or position.

Very often, newcomers look for a big victory—a major undertaking, a master plan, an accomplishment or innovation that has great significance. But these complex matters often take a fairly long time to plan, to persuade, to implement. Important as they are, it generally pays to establish yourself, even in a relatively small way, as soon as possible—demonstrating a "can do" approach, initiative, or creativity; solving a long-standing irritant; and so on.

In Chapter 88, I describe a parking garage "crisis." The solution to the problem was not a major breakthrough in intellectual thought, but it did indicate early on that the decision maker who was new would get things done and thus build a reputation and momentum for more difficult tasks and decisions ahead.

Thus, the task for the newcomer, president, vice president, department director, financial analyst—individuals at all levels—is to look for opportunities to make your mark, early on. It could be a matter of substance or a matter of style. For example, communication and interaction may be poor or nonexistent between one unit or division or another. You may want to go out of your way by word and personal action to demonstrate your concern for improving interaction and communication (meet the other people, get invited to their meetings, attend social functions, etc.). There may be various bottlenecks, delays in administrative processing or in production or shipping that can be easily solved by focusing on the problem, bringing people together to work on situations, changing procedures or practices.

The advantage of being the new person is that you can ask the simple questions as to why certain things are done or not done and, as a fresh pair of eyes, perhaps find simple solutions or pose the question differently so that people can suggest improvements or changes. Are overtime or delays, increased costs, frustration caused by how certain things are done? Perhaps there's a better way of doing them or perhaps a certain task need not be done at all or combined with other tasks, or job assignments made differently or work and workers organized differently or responsibility enriched and/or enlarged thereby enhancing effectiveness and efficiency.

As a newcomer, you are likely to have people at various levels come to you to identify problems. On the other hand, if you are new in a position, it is wise to reach out to supervisors, peers, subordinates, those with whom there is interaction to ask questions about how you can be helpful to them, meet their needs, be successful. The discussion will identify possibilities for small, quick victories which can then lead to larger victories that need not be as quick. This approach will enable you to make your mark early on, thus launching you to even greater successes.

42

WATCH OUT FOR BEING ONLY ONE DEEP

A colleague used to explain, in frustration, when faced with many important deadlines, "Boss, I'm only one deep!" Indeed, he was a one-man show, performing a variety of important tasks with no backup or assistance other than some secretarial support.

It is not unusual in a career that you serve for awhile as a one-professional-person unit or function, particularly during an era of downsizing. Your unit might have been a two- or three-person unit but is now down to one. Or, you may be part of a larger unit but have such a specialized function that in effect you are the only person carrying out that function, the only one really knowledgeable about it, and thus one deep in producing the service or skill required.

This type of arrangement has risks for the organization. What happens when you are on vacation, or ill, or demoralized because of too much to do (or perhaps too little to do) or too narrow a job, or when you are promoted or transferred to another job (or want to be) or leave, or retire? For the individual, there is the question of how to get your work done in a timely manner when you have to do all aspects of a job including those that you don't like and that may be at a much lower level. How do you benefit from the satisfaction of exchanging ideas with colleagues involved in the same specialty and get not only professional benefits but personal benefits of having interaction with colleagues?

When you find yourself in such situations or likely situations (or when farsighted organizations see the possible negative aspects of one-deepness both for the individual and the organization), it is important to seek ways to overcome the negative effects. This may involve seeking to enlarge and enrich the job to provide greater variety and challenge but also the opportunity to join a larger unit and then allow for cross-training so that more than one person is able to deal with the tasks. Being in a narrow one-deep specialty for a long time might be harmful to career growth and advancement and therefore you might well want to have an understanding with your supervisor as to the duration of the assignment, of how it can be broadened in the future.

It is good to feel that you are the one person who is in charge, the only one who can do this special function, but be careful; being one deep can hurt you professionally and lead to a great deal of dissatisfaction.

43

WINDING DOWN OR GEARING UP—DO NOT GO QUIETLY INTO THE NIGHT

———— ❧⚶❧ ————

At some time, different for each of us, the end of our career is in sight. Note, the end of a person's career is not the end of that person's life! Each of us has some idea or goal of a retirement age—50, 55, 60, 62, 65, 70, 75, never, or whatever other number strikes your fancy. Economics, health, interest in what we are doing, lifestyle, and whether we have a choice or not all influence when we retire.

But, retirement should not come upon us: Like other aspects of a person's career and life, thinking and planning are required well before the event. Financial advisors will tell you that financial planning for retirement should begin 20 or better yet 30 or more years before retirement. Progressive companies begin retirement counseling 5 or 10 years or more before usual retirement ages.

Aside from the obvious financial planning aspects of retirement, the less obvious and equally or even more important aspects involve questions concerning what you are going to do with your time. All of us have attics (or the equivalent) that we have longed to clean up, repairs to be made around the house, books we have always wanted to read, a language or a musical instrument we have wanted to learn, or become more proficient at, trips and courses we wanted to take, hobbies or interests we have wanted to take up or spend more time at, volunteer work, movies, plays, videos, museums, cultural pursuits we have wanted to see or do.

For many people, most or all of these pursuits are undertaken with great zest and enthusiasm, in addition to the joy of sleeping later and more and staying up later on occasion because of not needing to go to work the next morning. But also for many people, six months, a year, or two years later, the joy of retirement seems to wane.

Financial worries could beset us or the pressures of being around a spouse or significant other much more, or the loneliness of not having someone to be around and no job to go to. Even if these do not occur, the major issue is how do we fill the more than 40 hours a week formerly spent at work (for many, counting commutation time and time spent on work in an overtime fashion or on weekends, the time to be filled might be 60 or more hours a week). Not only is there a question of filling the hours, but filling them in a satisfying way.

Further, there is a fundamental question that must be faced. For many individuals, particularly males, their jobs have defined them as people. What they do provides them not only with status and a sense of worth but also many of their personal relationships, (women, in general, are much better in forming relationships on and off the job). Take away the job and a lot more than income is taken away. Indeed, for some, the reason for their existence is now in question and retirement just appears to be a waiting period for death—perhaps a long, lingering, and painful death.

As individuals and as organizational officials, we need to focus on the psychological aspects of retirement by preparing ourselves and our colleagues for the next stage of our and their careers and lives— the nonformal work stage. Those who enjoy their retirement get involved in the various aspects and pursuits listed earlier in a carefully planned way and make a combination of those activities their new "career" or "job" but without the pressures and stress of a job. Their goal is fulfillment, satisfaction, pleasure for themselves; and, for some, providing service, assistance, and pleasure to others.

To achieve our goals in this aspect of our careers, we need to plan for the retirement stage of our lives. This involves knowing ourselves and what gives us pleasure or what we think will give us satisfaction and fulfillment. Years ahead of our retirement date, we need to begin to explore hobbies, interests, activities, volunteer involvements, part-time business as work opportunities that would provide enjoyment and fulfillment so that we achieve more than just filling time. The person who has just retired at 65, 68, or 70 and presents him- or herself at an organization or institution saying, "Here I am, what can I do to help?" may be valuable and may end up providing help and being helped. But it would be better for the individual and the organization if, years before, he or she had become involved in some way, perhaps a small way. That involvement would more likely lead to a more fulfilling and valuable experience for the individual and the organization in those retirement years.

In essence then, winding down also involves gearing or winding up for the next stage of your life and career. This next stage may very well last, assuming reasonably good health, 10, 15, 20 or more years, equal perhaps to time spent in your last job or career. Just as you have spent time and effort preparing for and managing your career, the same kind of preparation and effort should go on during the winding-down stage as you prepare for what can well be among the best years of your life.

44

WHEN PLANNING AND IMPLEMENTING CHANGE, CONSIDER BOTH REVOLUTIONARY AND EVOLUTIONARY APPROACHES

Change is an important factor in the success of an organization and in its ability to meet new challenges and opportunities. The forces and factors bringing about the need for change can be either internal or external or both.

Internally, changes in mission, key staff, bottom-line results, staff turnover, sales, productivity, product returns, community relations, accidents, morale, and production line flow and speed may all be indications that changes or refinements in policies, procedures, and practices are necessary. Externally, factors include competitive standing, innovations, actions, and status of competitors, suppliers, distributors; governmental actions; economic conditions and climate; and international conditions and affairs. Numerous conditions outside the company's control can affect operations—mail, telephone, shipping and distribution, weather, and other factors that influence supply of materials necessary for success and demand for the organization's goods and services.

Whatever the cause or combination of causes and needs, at some point the leaders of the organization decide that it is necessary to make a significant change or series of significant changes. The issue then is in planning for change and in implementing the plan, should a revolutionary or evolutionary approach be used? By revolutionary, I mean the decision to make radical or very major changes quickly and decisively. The evolutionary approach introduces change gradually on a phased-in basis and may not have a complete plan or timetable in mind at the beginning but seeks to evaluate the impact of one phase or series before going further.

Whatever the approach, involvement of those concerned is vital, not only to get those affected "on board" early and to seek to get them to "buy in" to the solution and support it, but also because their ideas and advice can be of great importance to the success of the undertaking.

There is no one preferred approach, it depends on the circumstances faced, the capabilities and style of individuals, whether time is of the essence (the organization may be well on the way to extinction). There need not be one pure approach, certain aspects of the plan can be dealt with in a revolutionary way, others in an evolutionary manner and there are various combinations. The plan may be revolutionary and the implementation evolutionary, the plan evolutionary and the implementation revolutionary.

Planning and implementing significant changes involve great and careful effort; attention to detail; contingency plans; anticipation of what could go wrong and how to react; careful and thorough communication, briefings and training and retraining of those affected; the careful and timely introduction (if applicable) of new equipment, techniques, tools, procedures, practices, and sometimes a change in an organization's culture.

If the changes necessary are of sufficient importance, care must be taken to maintain focus on the issues and the approaches. It is easy to go off on tangents and be diverted by other concerns or by outcries against the effects. But a laserlike focus must be maintained.

If conditions, new information and ongoing evaluation warrant, modifications, large or small, can be made in the plan and in the rev- olutionary/evolutionary philosophy and approach. But one should not shy away from the quick, decisive action—selling off a division, shutting a plant, cutting the workforce appreciably—if careful con- sideration has led to that conclusion, despite the outcries. On the other hand, one should not be rushed into the most extreme action, the "macho" response, if more evolutionary approaches seem to offer the best solution to the problem.

45

THE MOTIVATING FACTOR—HOW LEADERS INSPIRE ADMINISTRATORS

Administrators in general, or in staff or "back office" departments and functions, sometimes fall prey to believing they are unknown, unappreciated, undervalued, undercompensated, and underused. This feeling can strike anyone from entry-level professionals to de- partment directors to even some vice presidents. Though they know that their work supports all of the organization's activities, they may not be directly involved in the primary missions of the organization and are thus relegated to the status of "support" staff. Many admin- istrators feel they are second- or third-class citizens.

SENDING MIXED MESSAGES

How staff-back office administrators are compensated is a major issue, for it affects both monetary and psychic rewards. In some cases, experience has led some administrators to believe:

- Their compensation packages are based on whatever is left over after other budgetary needs are met.
- When budget cuts are made, they receive lower percentage increases than other groups receive (unlike clerical or maintenance staffs, administrators do not have unions to advocate on their behalf).
- Their salaries are among the first to be frozen.
- Their positions or the staff in their areas are the first to be reduced.

They also feel uninvolved in some of the broader, more difficult, and more interesting problems facing the institution, since they may be viewed as narrow specialists.

Beyond the external factors that may affect how an administrator feels about his or her work are internal ones relating to perceptions of self-worth. The administrator may wonder:

- Is he good at what he does?
- Is her function or unit important and necessary or performing at more than a satisfactory level of competence?
- Does he or she measure up intellectually or productively to those who have more education, more recognition, and more hard evidence of their accomplishments?

Add to these, the concerns of a midlife crisis, burnout, boredom, or a sense that personal growth has peaked and you have a recipe for administrative frustration and dissatisfaction.

Assuming the complex challenges facing organizations now and over the next decade will require them to improve their effectiveness, inspiring the entire professional staff to achieve their maximum potential is vital to the leadership of presidents and vice presidents.

Many administrators have been around the organization and their specialty a long time. They have specialized skills, but are concerned and have something to contribute beyond their specialty, department, or even beyond the administrative area itself. Also, in the past decade, they've been able to benefit from considerable growth in the levels of professionalism, knowledge, skill, and training in their areas. As a result, experienced administrators have much to contribute, even beyond their current tasks, if sensitively asked and fairly recognized and compensated.

The best staff and support administrators seek to be treated as professionals very much interested in and dedicated to the organization. Institutional leaders must seek more ways to use administrators' talents and to make them feel rewarded both monetarily and personally.

Following is a list of actions to motivate, recognize, and make better use of administrators. While some of these suggestions are based on principles of good management that should be embedded in the president's mind, they bear repeating. With the stress and demands of leading our complex institutions, it is easy to forget that our greatest resources are the human ones.

PROVIDING FINANCIAL REWARDS

In regard to monetary compensation, leaders should review their policies and consider the following approaches:

1. *Use a merit system to make compensation decisions.* Base performance evaluations on a management-by-objectives approach and use tough, yet fair, standards of evaluation. Peg increases to levels of performance and be sure there are sizable differences between salary increases for unsatisfactory, below average, average, above average, and outstanding ratings. A 0.5 to 1.5 percent difference, for example, is not significant.

2. *Make sure the salary pool treats back office/support administrators equitably.* Average percentage salary increases for administrators should be the same or close to those for others in the organization. In extreme cases, supervisors may be earning very little more than subordinates (in fact, with overtime pay, subordinates might earn more).

3. *Emphasize internal promotions.* Do not make promotions in title only; make salary increases significant.

4. *Recognize new responsibilities with salary supplements.* At times, individuals take on significant, ongoing responsibilities

that are not great enough to merit a promotion or position up-
grade. Recognize the person's additional effort and responsibility
by supplementing his or her salary for as long as the responsibilities are held. Alternatively, if the responsibilities can be considered a permanent aspect of the position, merge the supplement
into the base salary.

5. *Provide an equitable benefits package.* The employee benefits
   program and employer contributions policy for administrators
   should be generally similar to those in more noticeable positions.

RECOGNIZING AND MOTIVATING

No budgetary considerations restrict nonmonetary compensation,
so there are plenty of options for making administrators feel valued.
Stress meeting individual needs for recognition, esteem, and self-
actualization; demonstrate understanding of the importance of the
individual administrator and his or her unit and the entire administrative area; and provide outlets for the administrator's ideas, energies, and interests.

Even for staff further down the career ladder, the president, vice
president, and at times, the chair of the board of directors should be
involved in providing such compensation.

Consider these approaches:

1. *Let the spotlight shine.* Share the credit. See that the names of
   major contributors to the success of an undertaking are put on
   or in the report. Mention their contributions in appropriate
   publications, meetings, and newsletters. Publicly and privately
   give them the credit and praise that is rightfully theirs. Encourage those who made major contributions to a report, project,
   innovation, or system, to make presentations to you and to various groups: the cabinet, the board, and governmental bodies.

2. *Solicit ideas, suggestions, and advice.* Solicit administrators'
   ideas not only in their specialty, but in broader areas, and beyond their usual concerns. Encourage brainstorming sessions
   and retreats.

3. *Broaden involvement.* Place various staff administrators on committees, planning groups, and project teams even if these do not usually have administrators as members. They will be able to contribute different perspectives while broadening their own.

4. *Use the management-by-objectives approach.* Ensure that the management-by-objectives evaluation system emphasizes full employee involvement in setting unit and individual goals and in evaluating results.

5. *Focus on job enrichment, not just job enlargement.* Often people feel their learning curve has slowed or stopped, and that they have reached a plateau. This is a particular problem at small organizations. At times, all you can hope for there is that your vice presidents, directors, and assistant directors will serve you well for three to five years before going on to other positions to enhance their careers. Big is not necessarily better, but many people believe they must go on to larger places to earn more money and prestige. To counteract this feeling, look for ways to expand learning, growth, and responsibility.

   You might have to violate good organizational charting and grouping of responsibilities to take advantage of an individual's skills and knowledge and to provide growth in responsibility and salary. Focus on giving individuals a sense of autonomy, of being in command of themselves and their area (under general guidelines), and of being able to make significant decisions.

6. *Stress communication—upward as well as downward.* Let people know early—before information is public or in the rumor mill—what is going on. The president or appropriate vice president should have one or two group meetings a year with all administrators to discuss the organization and to respond to questions. Also, encourage upward communication. Listen. Have an open door, ear, and mind. Encourage people to share with you their hopes, frustrations, and concerns. Likewise, provide opportunities and channels for individuals to express dissatisfactions and grievances.

7. *Initiate awards for outstanding administrative accomplishments.* Establish one or two awards for administrators,

perhaps one for creativity/innovation and one for outstanding performance.

8. *Encourage professional development.* Provide opportunities and cost reimbursement to attend conferences, courses, workshops, and degree programs. This promotes learning, informal discussions and networking, relaxation, and a change of pace. In order to promote from within as well as to provide opportunities for employees to learn and grow, you might also create a training and development plan for each administrator that includes courses, workshops on and off campus, and on-the-job training.

9. *Be concerned about employees who overwork.* Too many of your best and brightest administrators simply work too hard and too long. You should encourage them to keep reasonable hours and use their vacation time. But you may have to prepare to increase staffing in overloaded units and lessen your demands on certain individuals and units by delegating to others or by adding staff.

10. *Invite administrators to meetings and events.* The events could be social, cultural, academic, ceremonial, or athletic.

11. *Express appreciation where and when appropriate.* Don't cheapen praise by using it lavishly or too frequently, but when it is deserved make sure the individuals (and their supervisors) know that you appreciate their efforts. Whether the commendable action is directly related to the individual's job, service on a committee, something beyond job requirements, or to activities off the job, write a letter, make a phone call, or stop by to say thank you and to commend.

12. *Involve staff administrators in joint undertakings with line administrators and other groups.* In addition to the activities previously indicated, there could be clubs, social/cultural/athletic events, athletic or recreational sport teams that involve combined membership in friendly competition.

13. *Make appropriate allocation of funds for new office furnishings, equipment, painting, and remodeling.* Often staff administrators below the vice presidential level are low on the list when funds are available for making the office environment

more attractive and modern. This can be a source of dissatisfaction and should be rectified.

14. *Recognize milestones.* Hold annual events for employees who have reached the 10- or 20-year mark; send letters (and gifts if possible) at any significant anniversaries of employment (5, 10, 15 years, etc.). Encourage supervisors to acknowledge birthdays as well, with a card or lunch.

15. *Get to know individuals.* Take time to talk about nonwork matters; invite subordinates and colleagues to lunch, for a drink, coffee, or an informal meeting just to talk. Indicate sincere interest in them.

16. *Find out what staff administrators are thinking.* Use the human resources staff or hire consultants to interview people. Have supervisors set aside time to talk privately with individuals about their needs, goals, and aspirations.

PROVIDING STRONG LEADERSHIP

Finally, in motivating and raising the morale of administrators, nothing is more important than strong leadership. All of us respond to those individuals who, by attributes of mind, character, personality, and style, can inspire us to greater heights, to reach beyond ourselves. Not all of our organizations can be the best or in the top 10 percent in their industry, but all institutions, departments, and individuals can strive to be better than they are today. The personal example of presidents and vice presidents—their dedication, high standards, integrity, and concern for people and results—can provide role models for everyone in the organization. We sometimes forget the profound effect on morale, motivation, and performance of dedicated, visionary leaders.

I have outlined some of the basic actions that can encourage top officials and those who feel undervalued and underused to focus on the problem and some solutions. The administrator can talk to his or her supervisor, the human resources department professionals, spouse, friends, professional counselors and so on to identify the problems and create a workable plan to overcome them.

On the other hand, the president and vice president can indicate their strong desire to encourage growth, involvement, and recognition. These leaders should be asking: Whose judgment, knowledge, and dedication do I value and how can I use these individuals' talents more fully?

All organizations need all the talent they can get to improve their effectiveness in meeting the formidable challenges they face now and in the future. We must not overlook the talent, dedication, and knowledge of the people already at the institution and the significant contributions they can make.

We come to the end of this section of the book after having tried to help you focus on those things that will improve your style so that you are successful in regard to financial results, productivity, and people—immediately, and short and long range. The bias has been not to make you a good or bad guy, tough or easy, but rather on becoming an effective practitioner of management who has the style to reach the top.

II

MANAGEMENT SKILLS

46

THE LIGHT AT THE END
OF THE TUNNEL

It's only natural toward the end of a tough project, implementation plan, analysis, or fiscal year that you begin to look and hope for the light at the end of the tunnel. Things have been rough and tough; you've been working very hard and fighting adverse situations and conditions with all the mental abilities and physical stamina you have. Either because the crisis or challenge is ending or you hope it will be ending, you begin to think "just two more weeks (12 more tasks) and this will be all over . . . or the end will be clearly in sight."

The ability to see the finish line or to see the curve that leads to your destination approaching, is a great motivating force. It's like the "bell lap" in a long race; you know that you're in the final lap and you can use your remaining stamina in an all-out effort to win and set a new record. The ringing of the bell, the sight of the curve, that search for the light at the end of the tunnel—all serve to motivate, to provide a surge of energy and enthusiasm to reach your goal or destination. In fact, without that boost, you sometimes wonder how you would ever have achieved or completed what you did.

All of this is very beneficial. We all need benchmarks, milestones, and intermediate goals to reach and conquer and to provide the impetus, challenge, and reward for us to carry on. Given the hard fight, it is only natural that we eagerly look forward to a triumphant finish or at least to finishing the task before us.

Just at this time, however, there is the danger that we will let up or let down our attention or guard for a moment and seek to coast in or struggle toward the finish without being fully aware of problems we might face. In a similar way, the front runner in a race may keep an eye on the finish line and not pay enough attention to the competitor who is maneuvering to pass, or the champion boxer may be coasting along in the 15th round looking toward the final bell when he gets hit with the knockout blow.

Thus, no matter how tired you are—physically and mentally—and perhaps even how bored you are with the task, you must keep your attention up and push yourself not only to complete the task, but to complete it in style—not struggling to the finish line, but reaching it in full stride. You can be doing excellent work all along and then throw it all away at the end by, in one way or another, letting your guard down. If you do, the light at the end of the long tunnel won't be what you've been waiting for, but will be another train, on the same track, heading straight for you.

47

WHERE YOU STAND DEPENDS ON WHERE YOU SIT

Rufus Miles developed the law "where you stand depends on where you sit." In essence, your viewpoint as to the approach, consequences, and solution of a problem or even your perception of reality will depend on the view you have of the situation, which is based on your vantage point in the organization. The teacher who is promoted to assistant principal, the person on the assembly line who becomes a foreperson, the noncommissioned officer who becomes a commissioned officer, the union president who becomes a manager, the lawyer who becomes managing partner, the specialist who becomes a supervisor—these and similar promotions will bring changes in perception, view, and approach. Different levels of management will view things differently, based on the scope and breadth of their responsibilities and the view that they have of the organization and its needs. The view of problems and implications from the corner office of the top executive floor of the building differs from that of the middle-level manager with an obstructed view outside his or her window, and this view differs from the person who has no windows at all in his or her office, who, in turn, sees things differently from the person with no office!

What's important, what's the real problem, how to approach problems, short- and long-range implications of particular actions—all these and other actions in management call for different perspectives from various people, depending on their positions and breadth of responsibilities as well as their own abilities. Although you want a clerk in the returns department to be friendly, courteous, and helpful, you don't want him or her to be overly liberal in accepting returns. On the other hand, you may want your manager of the department to be more understanding of customer complaints. The leader of a militant faction in the union who becomes president may find it important to modify positions to unite the union and enable it to deal effectively with management. The outstanding researcher who has just become director of research is now concerned not only with the freedom and resources available as he or she was previously, but also with questions of productivity and the bottom line.

Successful fast trackers, at every stage of their climb, will want to sharpen and broaden their perspectives beyond the strict confines of their particular positions, while not overlooking the demands of their current positions and the primary focuses of their analyses and advocacy. They must represent their departments or study teams' viewpoints, but must be broad enough to have these views not too narrow or myopic. In dealing with others, they will recognize that Miles's Law holds true for most people so that their goals are to understand that and be prepared to attempt to broaden others' views or to attack them for being too narrow. On the other hand, successful advocacy will take into account the need for perspective. Thus, I would argue, fast climbers modify the line to: Where you stand depends on where you sit and hope to sit.

48

SUCCESS COMES TO THOSE WITH A HIGH TOLERANCE FOR AMBIGUITY AND FRUSTRATION

Textbooks and teachers often do not emphasize sufficiently the relatively large amount of ambiguity and frustration that exists for many positions. Despite organizational charts and manuals, position descriptions, company objectives, policies, plans, letters, and discussions by supervisors as to what's expected, there is, in many cases, considerable ambiguity about duties, authority, relationship to others, and goals (even with management-by-objectives systems).

Sometimes the ambiguity is a deliberate organizational or managerial style: Keep things loose and flexible so individual initiative and creativity can flourish. Another reason is to protect oneself if something goes wrong: You didn't understand what I meant. Or, if directions are ambiguous, let's see who has the strength, creativity, and knowledge to make order out of what seems to be chaos or at least messiness. Or: I don't want to make a decision that upsets or downgrades some person or unit, so I'll be indefinite and let others draw their own conclusions or hope the problem eventually goes away. Finally, the decision maker may feel not sufficiently informed, intelligent, strong, or willing to take risks, and so deliberately does not clarify or act decisively but rather straddles the issue, normally in a barrage of ambiguous words and directions or by silence.

At times, the ambiguity is accidental. Those who are supposed to be providing clear directions just don't realize that what they say and do (or don't say or do) can be misinterpreted or that they do not provide sufficient, definite guidance and directions. It may be a matter of style, tone, or word usage, but somehow the intent and decision does not get across to those who should be acting on the decisions made.

When faced with ambiguity, you must learn how to seek out clarity, from whom, what signals to look for and follow, and which to discard. You must also learn when it is best not to attempt to clarify. Sometimes the explanation needed will not be available and you must seek to do the best you can based on as much information as you can get as well as your own perceptions of what is meant. You can play it safe and roll along for a while to see if clarification comes or how those higher than you are interpreting the ambiguous situation. At times, however, you will have to act on what you know and perceive and at least clear up the uncertainty for yourself and others for that particular instance. It is risky—you may be wrong. Then again, you may be bright and forceful enough to make your interpretation the one that becomes the accepted course of action that is followed by others. In essence, you cannot always expect clarity or consistency, logic and rationality, fairness and high integrity. You will have to learn to live and prosper in situations and organizations that are confusing and contradictory and that require you to navigate through waterways that are not totally or clearly charted.

Often, frustration is the result of ambiguity in an organization. But there are other causes of frustration for the individual and the unit. Policies, procedures, and practices may be burdensome, out of date, or plain wrong. Resources may be inadequate to meet needs. Planning may be inadequate or nonexistent. Interpersonal relations in the organization may be deteriorating. Your full talents and contributions may not be recognized, appreciated, or utilized. There may be staff turnover and absenteeism. The organization's competitive and financial position may be declining. Compensation arrangements may be poor. External and internal forces on the organization or unit may be causing significant morale problems and a feeling of job dissatisfaction. To further compound all of these, there may be the feeling that there is no light at the end of the tunnel, that things will just keep getting worse, and that no one is able or willing to turn things around.

Most of us should expect some frustration on the job for the reasons previously outlined or for the normal everyday reasons: Work isn't performed properly or on time, something breaks, someone is sick, the mail is delayed, or similar circumstances. We have to learn to deal with the usual annoyances and the major concerns or frustrations indicated earlier. This can be done by talking to yourself or, preferably, a spouse, friend, or colleague about what's eating at you. Just describing it to someone helps you separate what is annoying and frustrating but is not that important, is likely to go away, or is at least tolerable from those things that are indeed major. You can seek to deal with the light or minor annoyances by attacking them directly, getting used to them and not allowing them to bother you unduly, or laughing them away. The major frustrations will take more than positive thinking. You will have to determine what you can do about them and proceed to do the best and most you can. But if there is very little you can accomplish, despite your best efforts, you have to decide how much you can or want to take. There's no sense getting an ulcer or heart attack or being unbearable on or off the job because of the frustration and tensions in the job. You can learn to let things slide off your back by saying, There are some things I cannot change and I will do the best I can. Or you may conclude that this is just not worth causing professional, psychological, and maybe physical damage to yourself. In other cases, if you have the choice, you may find it best to get out of the situation.

Each person must decide how much ambiguity and frustration he or she can tolerate, though you should recognize that there will always be some. You will have to learn to deal with these realities of life through meeting some situations head on and attempting to remove or change the causes. In other cases, you will need to avoid or ignore the situations, slough them off, laugh them off, or learn to live with and tolerate them. If you can psych yourself up to deal with frustration and ambiguity without letting them affect you deeply, you will be amazed to see how much of the previously or newly upsetting things you can handle. In not getting thrown off course by these rather powerful forces, you will be a stronger, more successful executive.

49

KNOW WHEN YOU AND
OTHERS DON'T KNOW

———————— ✖ ————————

One of the best subordinates I have ever known was truly excep-
tional in ability, except for one thing: He didn't know when he didn't
know. For him, it was an issue of pride and ego. He was confident
that he knew everything about his area of responsibility down to the
most minute technical matter. It took me some time, and many mistakes, before I learned that good as he was, there were some things
his subordinates, and certainly outside experts, knew better.

As you climb the executive ladder, it is natural for you and others
to have increasing confidence in your breadth and depth of detailed
knowledge, analytical ability, judgment, and experience. But there
is no shame in admitting that there are some aspects of a problem or
decision that you need help with or about which you know very little or nothing. Sometimes this lack of knowledge can be overcome
by relying heavily on the advice of capable subordinates, colleagues,
or outside experts. Sometimes you may try to delay making a decision, hoping the problem will go away and, thus, your lack of knowledge and indecisiveness will not be displayed. (This will not work
very often, and still leaves you vulnerable.) Occasionally, you may
have time to attend briefings, training courses, and read materials
so that you gain some understanding of the area; but if it is a complex problem you may not have the time, background, or inclination
to become truly knowledgeable. If it is an area outside your general
responsibilities, you may want to indicate that someone other than
you should head the committee or task force.

In general, the best approach in terms of your own lack of knowledge is to begin, first, by admitting to yourself, I don't know or I
don't understand this fully or at all. Then you can decide which type

of positive action to take, rather than hoping something goes away. This will depend on the importance of the subject and the decision at hand or looming, the time frame for making a decision, your schedule, your interest and knowledge base, the availability and capability of subordinates and outside consultants, and the availability of various training means. You have to decide one way or another to become broadly knowledgeable and, if it is important enough, considerably knowledgeable. If you have good staff and consultants, you can ask probing questions beginning with, "I don't understand this at all. Will you please provide me with sufficient information so that I can grasp the issues?" You may want to bone up by exposure to basic background documents and then move on from there.

In regard to your subordinates, you should encourage a feeling that they should be honest with you in admitting when there are gaps in their knowledge or ability. You need accuracy, thoroughness, and informed judgment rather than guesses or desperate reaching for any solution. You can help your subordinates, yourself, and the organization by drawing up training and development plans for each subordinate (and yourself) and allocating funds to meet the needs. This would help in a general sense. But when a particular issue comes up before the knowledge gap has been closed, honesty is again important. You can offer to give the subordinate more time to get the information or knowledge, thus relieving some of the stress on him or her. On the other hand, if time is short, you may want to use a task force or problem-solving team approach, utilize other resources in the company or your unit, or employ outside consultants.

Knowing when you and others do not know helps you avoid dangerous errors and points the way to areas where increased knowledge and experience are needed. It requires honesty and self-confidence that says, "I don't know now, but I will manage to meet the issue and I am capable enough to learn so that I can meet similar issues in the future." This approach allows you to strengthen your subordinates and yourself. You will be able to maintain as an important objective in your organization an emphasis on continued learning and growth and keeping current with new and future developments, techniques, and opportunities in your field and industry.

50

Take "Principles" of Management with Grains of Salt

We have all been exposed to management principles that stress the science of management and imply that proper application of these principles will result in very high probability of success.

Some of these principle are:

Unity of Command. Each subordinate, situation, or condition should be under the control of one and only one immediate superior.

Hierarchy/Number of Levels—Scalar Chain. Each individual and unit is ultimately responsible through succeeding levels to the chief executive officer at the apex of the hierarchy. The number of levels should be kept as small as possible to facilitate control and communication.

Authority Can Be Delegated, Responsibility Cannot.

Authority Should Be Commensurate with Responsibility.

Duties Should Be Clearly Defined.

Span of Control. There is a limit to the number of subordinates an individual can supervise; that limit is, according to many writers, somewhere between 5 and 12.

Although these and many other principles have considerable validity, I suggest that they must be analyzed and applied by taking into account the particular organization and the problems and opportunities it faces now, short-term and long-term. In essence, there is both an art and a science to management and while the principles stress the scientific part, we must always recognize the art. In a way, the principles, as Herbert Simon suggested many years ago, can be seen as proverbs; one can find opposing principles and proverbs. I have tried to make this point in speeches and teaching by asking audiences and students to give me opposing proverbs. I frequently receive such contrasts as: "Absence makes the heart grow fonder—Out of sight, out of mind," "He who hesitates is lost—Look before you leap," "Too many cooks spoil the broth—Two heads are better than one." The most creative contrast I ever received was from a clergyman who suggested, "Thou shalt not steal—God helps those who help themselves."

The principles, in my view, are guidelines, but they can be and often are violated, sometimes for good reason, sometimes inadvertently. For example, unity of command is frequently violated since one secretary may provide service to two or more individuals of the same or different ranks in order to save money for the organization. Authority commensurate with responsibility often breaks down, and as a way of overcoming this problem, the matrix, task force, or project organization has been developed. The span of control principle that calls for a relatively small number of individuals reporting to a superior, would, in complex organizations, contrast with the belief that you should keep a very small number of levels in an organization.

The span of control principle itself is worth taking a look at since what I call a "numbers racket" applies to it. One frequently sees 4–7, 5–8, 5–10, 6–12, as the "right" number for those reporting to an individual manager, particularly at the higher levels. I suggest that there is indeed a limit, but it depends on a number of factors within an organization at a particular time. At different times, that limit might change. In deciding on the limit, one must always balance questions of effectiveness and efficiency in a very wide span of control versus questions of additional expense, number of levels, and control and communication issues in a very narrow span of control. I would argue that the span of control depends on the level of supervision; the abilities and style of the superior and the subordinates; type, size, and complexity of the organization; time availability of the superior; complexity of issues and speed of decision making required; communication and delegation techniques used; rate of change in and on the organization; need for personal contact with subordinates, and so on.

This just illustrates that in designing an organization or meeting a problem, it is important and valuable to know and understand what "proven" theories and principles of management apply to the case at hand. At the same time, it is equally important to recognize that an issue or problem generally cannot be resolved by simply applying the principle in a cookbook-recipe fashion. One must take into account the realities and peculiarities of the particular problem and organization in determining whether, how much, and how a standard approach principle can be applied. The organization's history, present and future prospects, personnel, competitors, resources, and internal and external environment all must be taken into account.

There are indeed very helpful principles of management, as autopsies of failed decisions and companies can frequently attest. But in today's competitive and changing managerial climate, one cannot go unquestioningly by the book—even this book!

51

EVALUATE YOURSELF AND OTHERS

Assessing subordinates' performance and potentials is an important aspect of any manager's job. At the same time, it is equally important to assess your own performance and potential and plan for improvements and corrective actions necessary. Various types of evaluation systems can be utilized, and it is fashionable in management to keep trying to devise the "perfect" evaluation and assessment instrument. I would like to emphasize content rather than the format of the evaluation and assessment.

In essence, in evaluating others you want to have mutual agreement on the criteria to be used, how and when they will be applied, how they will be communicated and discussed, and how corrective actions will be formulated, implemented, and evaluated. A good method is to develop and set specific important objectives of performance and results or improvements to be realized, measure results quarterly or semiannually, and modify and take corrective action if necessary. It is important in setting such objectives that the short-term and long-term implications be taken into account as well as the immediate and one-year-horizon objectives. In addition, the impact that certain results or decisions will have two, three, five, or more years down the road should be carefully evaluated. You should be tough on yourself in terms of what responsibilities you owe your subordinates in assisting and supporting their performances, development, and training. You should also be tough in terms of applying the criteria to your own performance.

Evaluation criteria differ for different positions in an organization and at different times in an organization's history. The following list shows possible areas of evaluation and assessment. Not all will apply to all positions, and for different positions or times the weights assigned may differ. In applying the criteria, you might wish one analysis for evaluation of performance and one for assessment of potential.

CRITERIA FOR EVALUATION

I. Accomplishments, Skills, Abilities

1. Performance and results achieved in relation to objectives and to difficulties faced. Relationship of results to immediate, short-, and long-term objectives.

2. Decision-making skills—timely, well thought-out, effective and efficient decisions.

3. Judgment.

4. Abilities and achievements in regard to planning.

5. Abilities and achievements in regard to organizing.

6. Abilities and achievements in regard to staffing.

7. Abilities and achievements in regard to budgeting.

8. Abilities and achievements in regard to innovating.

9. Abilities and achievements in regard to communicating.

10. Abilities and achievements in regard to representing.

11. Abilities and achievements in regard to controlling.
12. Abilities and achievements in regard to directing.
13. Professional and technical skills.
14. Emphasis and results in regard to effectiveness.
15. Emphasis and results in regard to efficiency.
16. Emphasis and results in regard to economy.
17. Quality and quantity of personal work.
18. Quality and quantity of unit's work.
19. Professional growth.
20. Relationship with superiors, peers, subordinates, and those outside the organization, for instance, suppliers and customers.
21. Development of subordinates.
22. Sets high performance and personal standards for himself or herself and subordinates and motivates himself or herself and others to meet them.
23. Meets priorities and deadlines.
24. Evaluates issues from a broad as well as specific perspective.
25. Management of personal time.
26. Reporting to and briefing supervisors and others on problems, action taken, or to be taken.
27. Successful involvement in committees, assignments, and issues not necessarily limited to one's primary responsibilities.
28. Ability in regard to public/community/governmental/industry relations.
29. Keeps on top of developments in field, organization, industry.
30. Progress over the last rating period.

II. Attributes and Traits

1. Self-confidence.
2. Intelligence.
3. Ability to influence, inspire, motivate.
4. Ambition; desire for responsibility; desire for success.
5. Maturity in judgment, action, style.

6. Courage; decisiveness.

7. Integrity; honesty; ethics.

8. Handles stress, tension, frustration, victories, and defeats well.

9. Articulate.

10. General attitude—cooperative, congenial; has team spirit, zest, and enthusiasm.

11. Vigor; vitality; stamina.

12. Dependable; diligent; accurate; thorough.

13. Concern for results.

14. Concern for people.

15. Action oriented.

16. Dedication; commitment; loyalty.

17. Appearance; mannerisms; habits.

18. Flexibility in thinking and action.

19. Social skills—ability to work harmoniously with others.

20. Commitment to equal opportunity—affirmative action.

By devoting time and thought to these criteria and by formulating and implementing plans for improvement, you will be upgrading the performance of your staff as well as your own performance.

52

GRAPPLE WITH THE GRUBSNIGS

There are, in each organization, factors, forces, and constraints that can be regarded as potential demons. They can impede, delay, dilute, destroy, modify, and mangle the introduction, implementation, and lasting effect of changes in goals, policies, and practices. I have identified them as the GRUBSNIGS.

The GRUBSNIGS serve as a reminder as to where you should put a good deal of your time and energy. A lack of sufficient attention to any of them can cause significant problems for the organization and possibly for you.

Goals. Be clear and specific as to your immediate, short-, and long-term goals and develop the policies, practices, and plans for implementation and evaluation of progress and results.

Resources. Make sure you have assembled the resources necessary to accomplish your goals—human, financial, equipment and plant, technology and systems—and keep evaluating and upgrading these resources. In each resource area, you are concerned with getting and keeping the best you can afford, using to the maximum the potential contribution of each resource in an area (for example, in your human resources, you want to attract and retain the best people by concern for their compensation, job challenge, content of the position, psychic income, and work environment) and the interrelationship among resources.

Unions. Your management will be affected by whether or not you have a union. If so, what kind and what are your relationships to the union? Thus, you are concerned with the environment and issues that may lead to unionization and how to deal with those or, if unionization occurs or already exists, how to live with the union.

Budget. What you budget for and the budgeting systems employed are of great importance to the success of the organization. The budget is essentially price tags put on priorities. The basic issue is seeing to it that the budget reflects your goals and priorities and that the system utilized allows decision makers at various levels to see the choices available and how these fit into overall goals and priorities.

Systems. Considerable concern must be placed on having cost-effective systems that provide you with the results you wish in an effective, efficient, and economical manner. This concern would apply to efforts in the area of production, information, marketing, sales, budget, personnel, finances, general administration, and so on.

Near Term and Far Term. It is easy to get caught up in the crisis of the moment or month. There is a need to focus beyond the moment on the near- and far-term goals and objectives and how the actions of today and the near term contribute to achieving far-term results.

Information. You need reliable, complete, relevant, and cost-effective information quickly, in a useful form and format geared to management decision making and weighing of alternatives.

Groups. In planning and then taking actions, concern should be given to the involvement of the appropriate individuals and representatives of groups and to the effect of such plans and actions on individuals and groups. These may be groups within the unit or organization or outside the organization. They may be formal or informal groups within the organization.

Societal Concerns. What you and your company do and how you do it, your exercise of management style and skills—you should be concerned about how these relate to broader concerns of the local, regional, national, and even, at times, international community. Thus, equal opportunity and affirmative action, environmental, occupational safety and health issues, relationships and involvement with various communities, issues of integrity and fair practices, consumer-protection and customer-relations issues, the overall obligations of business to and in society—all of these are of sufficient importance to merit considerable attention.

By grappling with the GRUBSNIGS you will be able to deal with many of the major problem and opportunity areas you will face. Remember, the GRUBSNIGS need constant and serious attention, or they can cause you great harm.

53

TREAT TRIVIALITIES TRIVIALLY, OR, DON'T SWEAT THE SMALL STUFF

The TR³ Rule—Treat Trivialities Trivially—provides a valuable guideline for how you spend your time, energy, and emotions. Sometimes we lose sight of what we're trying to accomplish and what's important and in a sense take our eyes off the ball. We get distracted by those persons or issues that seem to shout more, cry out for attention, or that are annoying or never seem to be resolved. We get greatly upset because someone hasn't done something as quickly or as thoroughly as we would like, a report or brochure isn't quiet right, there's a delay in information or production, there has been some type of insult or lack of regard for us, personally, or to our unit, and so forth. These may be important and worthy of attention and action. On the other hand, these and many other issues may be of minor or negligible importance. You don't want to run a slipshod operation because sooner or later lack of attention to detail and too loose working standards and habits will cause significant problems. But, you also don't want to get personally and emotionally involved in minor nitty-gritty matters that eat up time and attention and create an atmosphere in which supervisors become finicky and obsessed with dotting every "i" and crossing every "t."

The difficult thing is to find the right balance between concern for everything being 100 percent right and the energy, emotion, and control systems that this will require—the balance between flexibility and rigidity. Certainly being too flexible, or not "sweating the small stuff" can create a problem of being too casual, can bring about an atmosphere of "good enough is good enough," and allow a lackadaisical approach to the job and its objectives. On the other hand, too much concern for having everything exactly right can create rigidities, slow down operations, inhibit creativity and new approaches, and result in a poor working environment.

Effective managers will be concerned about upholding high standards of performance and attention to detail (for instance, they should be very finicky about worker- and product-safety issues). However, they will seek to encourage in themselves and their subordinates an attitude of, Does this matter deserve the amount of attention, resources, and personal and emotional involvement I am thinking of putting forth? In many cases, the answer will be, Yes, but it will often be, No. As one looks back, it appears that a great many of the matters we got annoyed about were really trivial, but in dealing with them we utilized a disproportionate amount of time and emotion. Dealing with this issue is somewhat like the different situations facing a police officer on patrol. Sometimes the infraction the officer observes or is told about is so minor, or the situation is so unlikely to warrant investigation that it is better not to pursue it or even to slow down during patrol. Other situations involve the officer's needing to look more closely, to get involved slightly or in great depth, and some require the officer to draw a gun or call for reinforcements. When to act and when not to, how to avoid overreacting, when to place major priority or designate something as of major importance or a crisis, when to let something roll off your back, all involve judgment and experience. But, as one goes on "patrol," it is helpful to remember before going into action on any situation or letting something gnaw at you, whether the TR^3 Rule should apply.

54

SIMPLIFY THE COMPLEX; SEE THE COMPLEXITIES OF THE SIMPLE

The astute manager is able to understand situations so that he or she can get to the heart of the matter and focus on the essence of the issue or problem rather than getting caught up in secondary and diversionary issues.

In order to understand things better, he or she seeks to simplify the complexities of the issue, once the issue and its ramifications are understood, together with the alternative courses of action and their positive and negative consequences. Basically, this comes from emphasizing major objectives and goals, what the problem is and what it is not, and asking "Why?" "Why not?" "What?" "Where?" "When?" "How?" and "Who?"

By stressing simplification, and not a simplistic approach, he or she is able to cut through the underbrush and the various entangling branches and get to the core of the issue. This saves a good deal of time, energy, and cost. By continually stressing, "Let's not lose sight of the goals and objectives—the things that must be accomplished by our action rather than the things that would be nice to get accomplished," he or she is able to keep highlighting the essence of the problem.

Simplification also calls for breaking down the problem or issue into manageable parts, because in their enormity they can be overwhelming. Biting off chunks of the problem allows the manager to proceed on a timetable to reach solutions, to organize an effort, and to marshal and allocate resources. By solving the various parts of the problem, the manager brings everything together and brings the solution close at hand. He or she then focuses on presenting the issue and the effort completed to higher management with a stress on simplifying the complex so they can grasp the essentials quickly and easily. If the manager has done a good job in overseeing the solution of the problem and in presenting it to top management, he or she should have made the whole thing look easy. In fact, the neophyte in management might question, "What was all the fuss about?" since it would seem from the presentation so logical and simple to have reached a particular solution. The best managers have the knack of being able to simplify the complex so that it indeed looks simple and giving the impression that a solution or success was easily or relatively easily achieved despite enormous effort by all concerned.

The other side of this approach is that the good manager doesn't get overwhelmed by simplification. Depending on the problem and the individual in charge of dealing with it, there should be a concern that complexities may have been overlooked, avoided, or misunderstood. It is good to believe in the "face value theory." Namely, things are as they seem to be on their face. But, if it is an important matter, or a small matter that could blow up or steamroll into something bigger, the successful manager will seek to test out whether the possible complexities, hidden agendas, subtle ramifications, or possible, though not probable, consequences have been explored. Thus, he or she will review subordinates' work to see whether the "simple" presentation or solution covers whatever possible complexities can be seen, or that the solutions can be adapted to meet various contingencies.

By experience, power, and prestige, the good executive is able to simplify the complex and accomplish the goals sought. At the same time, he or she is able to anticipate and deal with the complexities in the seemingly simple.

55

BEWARE OF TOO MANY LEADERS, TOO FEW FOLLOWERS: EVERY ORGANIZATION NEEDS SOME GOOD AND RELATIVELY UNAMBITIOUS PEOPLE

In order to meet some issues and problems in management, we often need the equivalent of more privates and noncommissioned officers and fewer commissioned officers and generals. Furthermore, since leaders cost more (the costs for their compensation packages, perks, support staff, fancier and bigger offices, and so on, are considerably higher), we can find ourselves not having enough "troops" to accomplish the mission because a considerable portion of our resources have been spent on the leaders.

One of the failings of current American management is that we have emphasized and funded centralized staff and control functions so much that we have lost sight of the needs of the production line or sales force. Naturally, the centralized functions require college graduates, and preferably holders of MBAs, who cost a considerable amount. As they climb the corporate ladder, they advance and build their professional and support staffs. This may all be necessary, but on the other hand, it can easily be overdone. We can often find deputies, assistants, assistants to, and the creation or maintenance of small separate units so that more individuals can get or hold titles of director or manager, and of course, they have assistants and assistants to.

At the same time, we may be cutting down or out those who have to get the work done, hoping to replace them with computers or robots, improved systems and procedures, improved supervision, coordination, and communication. Certainly we will be able to utilize computers and technology to replace various types of low-skilled jobs. In fact, they may also replace some usual low- and middle-management jobs whose basic function was providing, transmitting, and communicating various types of information. Computers are not only a threat to blue collar workers, the are a threat to those with white collars, ties, and jackets!

We have to make certain that we have enough motivated and trained followers in all categories who are able to provide human skills and intervention in bringing about the goals, plans, and directives of the leaders. The engineer can analyze the problem, and two may be better than one, and three may not be necessary. But then you may need several people who can implement the engineer's solution and we must be careful not to skimp in seeing to it that they are available, motivated, and well-compensated.

Some people are very good, perhaps as good as or better than their supervisors or superior's superiors. But for a variety of personal reasons (or fate within the organization), they may have chosen to remove themselves from the race of climbing higher (or circumstances may have removed them). Some good people just do not want the headaches, heartaches, and tensions that go with competition for higher positions or for supervisory positions. Their goals, lifestyle, and personal satisfaction may allow or dictate that they remain in their particular areas and even the same positions. Often this happens to scientists, engineers, researchers, computer specialists, salespeople, and others who enjoy their particular responsibilities and do not want to go higher if that involves supervisory or managerial responsibilities or responsibilities different from their primary source of job satisfaction. Others, although in middle- or upper-middle-management ranks, may not want to progress further because of the demands and responsibilities that these higher duties will place on them. They are satisfied to perform well at the level they are serving.

For the organization, such people have real value. They perform well and do not feel unfulfilled or passed over if they have not advanced because, by and large, the decision has been theirs. The organization can have people of considerable competence and experience at highly skilled positions or in middle-management positions, thus strengthening an area that is vital to an organization's success. If one wanted to be humorous and possibly accurate, one could say that these good people have not fallen prey to the Peter Principle—they have not been promoted to their level of incompetence! There is some truth to this, because the individuals are likely not to perform as well in the higher positions.

To meet the issues described, it is important to see that the organization is structured and a climate created to reward talented followers as well as the leaders. The innovator and those who bear major responsibility, since they face the greatest pressures and risk, should receive just compensation and recognition. But, we should be careful not to overlook, either in compensation or recognition, those who helped make things happen by successfully following the leadership of others and performing well at their level of competence and satisfaction. They also serve well who stand ready to follow directives.

56

First-Rate Second Raters versus Second-Rate First Raters

One of the most interesting comments I have seen about someone applying for a position was, "He's a first-rate second rater." That raises the complex issue of whether, as individuals and organizations, if for one reason or another, we can't be or aren't assessed as being first-rate first raters, is it better to be a first-rate second rater or a second-rate first rater?

By first-rate first rater, I mean an individual who performs in an outstanding fashion in a very tough position in a high-standards, demanding organization that faces significant problems and competition. The individual is, in fact, playing in the major leagues, on a top contending team on which there are many excellent players—All

Stars or All-Star candidates at their positions, Superstars and almost-Superstars. In that group the person is able to hold his or her own and is considered one of the best players on the team. He or she is a star among the stars. A second-rate first rater should be considered as one playing on the kind of team described or in that type of organization—one who is considered competent but not outstanding; one of the weaker links on the team; one who tries hard but just isn't in the same category with most of the others. He or she may not be able to make the starting lineup or play well every day but is a good utility or fill-in player. The evaluation is not strictly in comparison with great individuals, but rather just on the basis of straight assessment of the individual's own performance and what is reasonable to expect. It is possible that in another organization the individual might do somewhat better because he or she would not face the psychological burden of feeling less competent than some of the others or would be perceived by others in a better light and, thus, would produce more.

A variation of the first-rate first rater is the organization that may not be that good or the industry that tough, but the particular demands of the position are such that it is indeed a first-rate position and the individual is meeting the demands in a superb manner.

(One could discuss the situation of a second-rate second rater, but there's not much that needs to be said about that other than that there are many such people around, and with good supervision they can make a solid contribution to an organization and also feel good about themselves.)

The basic and interesting contrast is with a first-rate second rater. Here we mean the individual who is performing in an outstanding fashion in a not-too-demanding job in a not-too-demanding organization and industry. To use the sports analogy, he or she is the best or among the best players on a noncontending major league team or a team in the high minor leagues. Although the individual is certainly considered very good or great in comparison to his or her peers on the team, or on noncontending teams, or in the minors, there's some concern whether he or she would do as well or well at all on a contending team or in the major leagues. Alternatively, the individual can be in a first-rate organization but in a less demanding division or position where he or she is performing very well but may not be considered up to handling responsibilities of the most demanding nature, or at the most would be a second rater if given further responsibilities.

In short, the issue is a variant on the old question of, Do you want to be a big fish in a small pond or a small fish in a big pond? But it also delves more deeply into evaluation of the individual.

Each of us must go through a very difficult, searing, introspective experience of deciding how much we have to give of ourselves, and whether we have the ability and drive to give it, in order to be a first-rate first rater. This may call for a degree of commitment, intelligence, drive, ambition, and sacrifice of self and family that we may not be able or willing to make. What it amounts to is, How much do you want to be one of the best among high achievers in tough and prestigious jobs in tough and prestigious organizations? How much psychic and monetary gratification will you get from being at the higher rungs in one of the best, if not the best, organization in your industry or in any industry? Some may recognize that they will never be, or be able to be, a first rater in the first-rate jobs or organizations, but are so stimulated by the challenges of such jobs and organizations that they will try to stick it out even if they are perceived by others and themselves as not of the same caliber as the first raters.

Alternatively, one can desire to do the best one can and indeed be outstanding in a job and/or organization that is rather mediocre. The job or organization may provide the style, pace, stability, location, security, and challenge that meets the individual's goals and desires and, thus, one feels fulfilled by being acknowledged as very good in what one does though one's position may not be all that important.

The first rater in a mediocre setting, the second rater in the outstanding setting may always wonder what would have happened if he or she tried for the tougher job or organization or dropped back to the less demanding job or organization. Would he or she have received more satisfaction? Would the second rater have held his or her own and been a star? Unless the individual tried it at some point and happily or unhappily settled or decided on something else, he or she will never know. For each of us, the decision is a very tough one, and in the end no one can really provide the answer. Circumstances and/or one's own self-study will determine at a particular point in time (and several years later the answer may be a different one) what is best for oneself or what one may have to deal with in regard to the issue of first-rate second rater, second-rate first rater, or that ideal world not often achieved of first-rate first rater.

57

UNDERSTANDING THE STARS— SUPER, SHOOTING, AND OTHERS

In the firmament of organizational life, one is on occasion exposed to stars and may have them as subordinates. Some are indeed superstars and take a permanent place, shining with great brightness, in the company's and sometimes the industry's or nation's galaxy. Others are more like shooting stars, rising very quickly, flying very high and fast, and then coming down very quickly, never to be seen or heard from again. A brilliant performance on an assignment or project, a major innovation, or a creative suggestion could be the cause of the rise of the shooting star. On the other hand, closer scrutiny and examination may reveal that the brightness of the star is shortlived, or that the particular performance is not repeated on other assignments. Thus, the former shooting star may sink into oblivion, perhaps remembered for that one brief moment, and may have left the company.

Another type of star is similar to Halley's Comet. The person flashes brightly and for some period, but then disappears for a long time, coming back from time to time.

Finally, there are varying degrees of stars that are spotted in the company's galaxy, sometimes easily and with the naked eye, other times with difficulty and only after a great deal of probing and investigation.

For you, the supervisor, colleague, or subordinate of one of the types of stars, it is important to know which type of star you are dealing with. Hitching your future to a shooting star is not terribly rewarding, while it certainly would be if you were to hitch onto the superstar or even a strong star.

Stars and superstars need care and an environment in which to flourish. The supervisor who has the courage, self-confidence, and talent to spot stars, to encourage them, and let them shine as brightly as they can is a great asset to the organization. It takes a good deal of humility and inner strength to recognize that while you are quite good and even a star in your own right, your colleague or subordinate may be a brighter star or even a superstar.

In essence, when dealing with long-lasting stars, the supervisor and the company have to seek ways to most completely utilize the contributions the individual can make by creating an environment that allows the star to shine brightly, thus contributing to the fullest extent possible. If it is a young person, new to the organization, you will need to serve as a mentor and help choose assignments and opportunities that develop his or her skills, knowledge, and exposure. It may involve serving as an advocate and smoothing the star's rough edges and approaches to problems and people, as many individuals feel threatened by highly talented, young, and ambitious people. If it is not a young college graduate with a bachelor's or MBA degree—someone with relatively little experience—but someone who has considerable experience, a different approach will be necessary. Here, you are more of a helpful colleague, exchanging ideas and knowledge, seeking to be of assistance in accomplishing your goals by utilizing the talent of the individual.

In both broad cases, you will need to share the limelight and glory with the greatest share going to the individual. However, as indicated before, your ability to nurture the individual and create a good environment allows the organization to reap considerable benefits. Each organization needs teamwork, but it also needs to develop and tap the brightest talent available and to allow those with unusual abilities to fly as high and as fast as they can without demoralizing others.

58

DEVELOP YOUR SUBORDINATES

Management writers frequently advise managers to make sure they have prepared someone to step into their place. This is supposed to demonstrate top-notch skills by developing others and making sure that the organization has capable heirs-apparent so that, in case of your promotion, leaving, or illness, the unit can be capably led. Furthermore, those higher in the company won't hesitate promoting you because your replacement is ready to step in, and so they know that they are not creating a major problem. Despite the sound advice, development of subordinates often is honored more in theory than practice. Some managers fear training their successors and letting them get known by higher officials because of a concern that they will be replaced by someone younger, brighter, more ambitious, and less expensive. Others like to prove they are indispensable by keeping their subordinates in the dark about other areas and broader issues within the unit. Some managers don't develop their subordinates because they just don't have the time or the knowledge of how to do so.

It is important for every unit within the organization to be concerned about horizontal as well as vertical training and development. As a manager, you want to have subordinates who have a high grade of skill in several areas and at least a reasonable level of knowledge and skill in other areas so that they can contribute on task forces or in joint planning and, if necessary, step into another role for a short period in case of an emergency. This is the horizontal aspect of training. It is similar to the military's primary military occupational specialty as well as secondary occupational specialties. Horizontal training can be accomplished through task forces and various joint problem-solving or issue-analysis approaches; through briefings by units to others about their work, problems, and achievements; by having individuals in units exchange jobs for brief periods—several weeks or months—so they get exposure and knowledge of different areas (job mobility); and by various company or educational institution training courses and by special assignments.

Vertical training can be accomplished by careful planning in providing opportunities for subordinates to perform one or more of their supervisor's functions. It will take self-confidence and trust on the supervisor's part, integrity, self-confidence, capability, and a sense of perspective on the part of the subordinate. The easiest way is to have people serve during the supervisor's absence on vacation or illness. But even when the manager is on the job, various responsibilities can be delegated, subordinates can accompany the manager to certain types of meetings or represent him or her at them; the manager can present a decision he or she is faced with and ask for the subordinate's responses giving critiques of the results. The manager can discuss fully the whole range of problems he or she faces on the job and get the subordinates' views before making a decision, and explain the reasons for the decision; the manager can encourage mobility assignments and training in various techniques and areas and in courses or programs given by the company or by universities. The manager can share tasks and responsibilities in which he or she would normally take the lead with subordinates or let them be entirely responsible. In presenting the subordinates' reports or briefings, the manager should allow them to get the major credit and a major share of the limelight.

The secure supervisor will want to use most fully the knowledge and ability of his or her best subordinates. They provide more highly skilled resources for the manager to use, thus increasing the possibility of improved performance in the unit and acclaim for both the manager and the subordinates. Letting the subordinates share the limelight frightens the insecure supervisor, but for the confident leader, it indicates to others that here is a manager who develops good people. This skill may get the manager promoted more quickly because he or she is leaving the unit in good hands, or at the least will gain the recognition that he or she is an outstanding manager who develops good people for the other slots in the company. Once the manager has shown a skill at doing this, it will not have been just the fact that he or she had a great subordinate that created a good performance, but the manager will become a highly regarded asset to any company. The capacity to recruit and select people with high potential and then to develop, train, nourish, and bring them along as quickly as possible—with a solid foundation being set—is a rare and valuable commodity in organizational life. The manager is also able to build loyalty and respect on the part of his or her subordinates and former subordinates that will help the manager's effectiveness in the company and industry, and in his or her own promotability.

The outstanding organization and executive truly believe in and devote time and resources to shaping the company and individual style and climate in order to encourage and develop talented individuals. This attitude yields a great return on investment for the company and the executive and builds the loyalty and job satisfaction among the most talented that is vital to the organization's present and future success. For the executive who is considering a serious commitment to development of his or her subordinates, remember, such action is not only important for them and the company, it is very good for the manager, as well.

59

IT TAKES MORE TIME TO DO THINGS THAN YOU HOPE, BUT LESS TIME THAN YOU THINK, OR, MEET YOUR DEADLINES!

Assuming high quality, the ability to accomplish things on time or early and to meet realistic yet tough deadlines is an important factor in success at all levels within organizations. What is to be accomplished can range from writing a simple memo that has to reach someone by tomorrow, to implementing a decision or taking action, to completing a major report or project. There will always be occasions that force you to miss a deadline through no fault of your own, such as natural disasters, equipment failures, transportation and information delays, unexpected illness or resignations, various bottlenecks caused by people, internal organization factors and actions by other organizations, supply shortages, economic and political conditions, and so on. A good planner will attempt to take into account some possible problems, assume that what could go wrong probably will go wrong, and make whatever contingency plans he or she can.

Leaving aside those things you cannot control or even anticipate, there are factors within ourselves and others that can lead to missing deadlines. Some people don't like to operate under the gun or the tension of having a specific date or time when something must be accomplished. They feel this constrains them, particularly in complex situations. Therefore, they will try to have the deadline as loose or long as possible or attempt to have the dates changed. Some will question how the supervisor reached a certain date, arguing that it was arbitrary, unrealistic, and not based on consultation.

In those cases in which you are the person who sets the deadline for others, it is important that you and the person who is being given the target date understand through frank discussion the importance of the assignment; the aspects of the assignment; the constraints or difficulties likely to be faced; the adequacy of responsibility, authority, and resources that have been or can be assigned; and what is expected. After a thorough discussion of these matters, a mutually agreed on target date can be developed. Usually you would want it sooner so that you have more time to review, can keep a reasonable amount of pressure on, can keep some time in reserve for emergencies, and will look good to your boss by being early or on time. The other person would want it later so that he or she has some leeway in case of unanticipated problems, is able to lessen the pressure on him or her, and to be able to look good if he or she is early. Through discussion, and especially after you have worked together on some assignments, a realistic time can be agreed on that is tight but not unreasonably harsh or unrealistic, which could lead to incomplete or shoddy work or missing the deadline.

Until you acquire considerable experience, it is natural to expect that you and others will be able to deliver a product rather quickly. Too much optimism in estimating comes from self-confidence, desire to impress, lack of full understanding of the difficulties inherent in the assignment or those that may arise, and a desire to motivate others and yourself by providing tough goals to reach. In time, your optimism will become realism but you must guard against pessimism. It is too easy to assume that things are much harder to do than they really are and if you fall into that trap, it will take you so long to deliver that you will hurt others in the organization or the organization itself in terms of its services, products, and competitive stance.

The experienced individual will make careful estimates of time needed using some variant of a three-level approach (breaking down the components of the task and providing estimates for each component): *optimistic* estimate as to time needed; *probable* time needed; *pessimistic* estimate of time needed. All of the estimates should be realistic and not assume either the absolute best or worst of all worlds. Certainly something disastrous or miraculous can happen that would put the actual completion date outside of the pessimistic-optimistic range, but one should assume that in 99 percent of the cases you will fall within the range. In developing the estimates, you balance your hopes, needs, and desires with what you know about the situation. Depending on the importance of the matter, from the very beginning it may be decided to devote more resources to the project in order to increase the probability of meeting a certain target date. Thus, target-date setting is an integral part of the planning process.

It is therefore helpful to ask: What is the latest date I have to complete this project? How do I build in some leeway for unanticipated occurrences? What must I give (or get) in order to meet my goals in terms of resources, authority, responsibility, and organizational approach? How do I motivate myself and others to achieve the goal? What reward or recognition is appropriate for success? (As a supervisor, you should be concerned about how you deal with a subordinate's failure to meet deadlines.)

At times, even the most careful plans can go astray for the reasons indicated earlier. Instead of sticking too long to original projections, corrective action should be taken immediately to deal with the changed conditions. This might require additional resources or changing the completion date with notification to others who are depending on the completion of the assignment. You have to balance the need to make a change in the date as soon as you know about the new situation versus the need to wait a while to get all the information in order not to have surprises that might lead you to change the date a second, or third, or fourth time.

Often, careful planning and anticipation and setting tough deadlines will lead you to overcome too optimistic a hope of completion, while also overcoming too pessimistic thinking about how much time you actually need to complete your assignment. The individual who can come up with realistic target dates and meet or beat them will soon develop a reputation as a "can-do" person. Such individuals are in short supply in any organization and are soon placed on the fast track to success.

60

OFTEN THE ONLY CERTAINTY IS UNCERTAINTY

We all feel more comfortable in making a decision if we have as much accurate information as possible. It makes us more secure to have the charts, graphs, numbers, alternatives, studies, reports, and computer printouts. At times, these materials, as well as a good deal of expert advice and background information, are available so that the decision maker believes that he or she has significantly reduced the risk in reaching particular conclusions.

Often, however, the certainty of information, "facts," clear alternatives, assessment of consequences is not all that certain. You may be sailing in uncharted waters—the development or invention of a new process, technique, product, or service. For competitive reasons or internal politics in the organization you may have to move secretly and quickly without having consulted widely or waited for all the information to come in or having done market research. The information you would like to have—in fact, must have—may not be available in the time period in which you must make a decision, no matter how many people you have working around the clock or whether you have the biggest and fastest computers at work. You may be able to get some of the facts you need totally, others partially, and others not at all. The information you are getting may spread more confusion than clarity since it may be coming in bits and pieces and be contradictory.

In short, quite often a number of factors cloud the ideal decision-making process and climate: time; availability of resources and information; capabilities and availability of key people; mental, physical, and emotional state of people; unanticipated events in the community, nation, or world (for instance, natural disasters, wars, strikes, too much or too little rain, and so on). The decision maker is often faced with having to decide without a high degree of certainty about the quantity and quality of the information necessary to ensure that the action he or she will approve is highly likely to be correct and successful.

Some decision makers keep searching for more facts and figures before they make a commitment. If you are making a choice that could cost lives or the independence of your nation, or millions, perhaps billions of dollars and lead to bankruptcy of the company, you need as much information, analysis, discussion, and thought as you can possibly get. But if you wait too long, events or the competition may pass you by.

The question then is: Assuming I have various degrees of discomfort with the information or views about a course of action, how and when do I decide? The answer really is, it depends on your tolerance level for discomfort, what it will take to make you more comfortable and certain, and whether you can afford to get it in terms of time, resources necessary, and the competition. In essence, you should condition yourself and your colleagues to get as much information as you can, emphasizing accuracy, thoroughness, and analysis of alternatives and consequences, and on the basis of what you have and the best judgment of the best resources available, you have to choose. You shouldn't try to hedge by splitting the difference; you make your best choice and overcome the normal paralysis of waiting for the ultimate degree of analysis.

We live in an uncertain environment. We try to bring order to things and to discern the order in things. But we must be willing to take some risks and substitute judgment for certainty.

61

SURPRISES ARE GOOD FOR PARTIES, NOT FOR MANAGEMENT

Surprise gifts, gags, and parties usually are great fun for those giving and getting them, except for surprises in management. Management cannot control the outside world and has difficulty enough controlling, planning, and anticipating within its industry and company. But, in all that it does, management attempts to prevent unpleasant surprises. It would even be willing to give up pleasant surprises if it could prevent unpleasant ones!

All deviations from norms or expectations cannot be anticipated. Sudden natural calamities; new products secretly developed by competitors; a strike in an industry that affects the supply or shipment of your raw materials or products; national or international economic, political, and military conditions; wildcat stoppages . . . the list can go on and on. If you had enough time and resources, you could develop or buy scenarios or descriptions of possible events that would have an important impact on your organization and then you could develop specific plans for dealing with these situations. However, the costs would be prohibitive. Even developing plans for dealing with the most likely happenings can be quite costly.

However, you need not be a small ship sailing in the ocean tossed around by every strong wave or wind. You can do some anticipation, recognizing that you will not be able to plan for everything and that things will occur that weren't foreseen at all or foreseen somewhat or very much differently. But some planning for contingencies beats no planning at all. And the more you do, the better you get at it and the greater your chances are for predicting and meeting the problems that arise.

The secret for surprise prevention is simply sound planning and anticipation and more sound planning and anticipation. For every organization and unit within it there ought to be contingency planning exercises and sessions devoted to "what if" questions. Computer simulation as well as brainstorming can be helpful. In essence, you are seeking to predict that what could go wrong, will, and then what you will do about it. Just as the military have contingency plans for various types of military actions and police plan for local disturbances, you will need to have such plans for all aspects of your business.

For every unit, whether it involves the flow of raw materials, production, marketing, shipping, quality control, public relations problems, or the like, it would be wise to have specific contingency plans drawn up with indications of who does what, when, and how. Who speaks for the unit or company, who takes over in certain situations, who has the authority to do what in certain emergencies? These plans have to be reviewed, updated, revised, and, where appropriate, rehearsed. They are, in effect, fire drills in management, where the safety and, possibly, the life of the organization can be at stake.

In addition to not wanting surprises on the big issues, you don't want to be surprised or embarrassed on smaller issues. Again, assume that what could go wrong will go wrong in such areas as funds available, organization and people, materials needed, external forces, facilities, equipment, technology, marketing and production, and so on. Thus, in reviewing a project, report, or plan, it is wise to anticipate what might go wrong and what modifications to the plan you would then make or how you would deal with the problem. You would want to assess possible reactions by others within and outside the company and take their reactions into consideration in developing your original presentation as well as your contingency plans.

You'll always get some surprises (some good, some bad) and that adds some zest and the spirit of the unknown to management. The approach outlined here, however, will minimize the number and impact of such surprises, thereby giving you greater control over your fate and that of your unit and organization.

62

REALIZE THE IMPORTANCE OF VIGILANT OVERSIGHT AND FLEXIBLE RIGIDITY

As a manager and executive, you should want to develop your subordinates and let them fly as far and as fast as they can. This is obviously good for them in terms of opportunity and motivation, and it is good for the unit and organization because talented people are encouraged to give their best. It is also very good for you because this type of attitude on your part will probably lead to greater creativity and productivity on theirs. This would help make the unit and you look good in terms of bottom-line results and the fact that you are a manager who develops subordinates and establishes high morale in a unit.

However, while you try to create a climate for creativity and delegation of authority, you must also recognize the importance of maintaining some degree of supervision and control and maintaining some basic principles that must be upheld. Thus, the challenge for you is how to maintain a balance between creativity and control, between giving maximum authority and responsibility to subordinates while still upholding your authority and responsibility. The same challenge exists at all levels within the organization.

I suggest that you consider adopting a management philosophy and practice of vigilant oversight. Note that I do not say "control," but the softer approach of oversight. (Of course, whether you can use this approach will depend on your competence, self-confidence, and personality, and similar aspects for your subordinates, the organization's history, present environment and style, and the problems and opportunities facing the organization.)

You will want a system that involves you in planning, in deciding on performance measurements, in evaluating results, in dealing with major crises and in the need for significant changes in plan. You will want to be kept informed generally as to progress and problems. The details of this approach can be worked out with your subordinates and may differ with various subordinates depending on your needs and concerns, their needs and concerns, and the nature of the problem. It can range from very light or little oversight to a rather strong system very close to a more formal control system. Whatever the degree of oversight (and remember you want to give maximum opportunity for talented individuals to run their own show), you want it to be understood that while it is oversight and not control—and it may be light oversight at that—you will be vigilant. You will be interested, concerned, involved, and available. You have not abdicated, but your approach is geared to maximum results and maximum opportunity for the individual in charge to show what he or she can do.

Another aspect of how you supervise and control is the degree of flexibility in terms of policies, guidelines, and practices to be followed by your subordinates. Some people believe in rigid flexibility; that is, they will deal with every situation separately and on an ad hoc basis. Although this promotes maximum discretion and creativity in meeting a particular situation, it raises severe problems in regard to precedent, whether there are any organizational standards, and what they are. Thus, I suggest that the principles, guidelines, standards, and practices be clearly and simply stated without ambiguity. In a sense, these should all be rigidly set forth. However, as situations arise, your subordinates should have some leeway and you should have more. After checking, if necessary, with your supervisor, you should be able to interpret policies and practices in as flexible a way as possible to meet the needs of the situation. This has to be done carefully so that it does not degenerate into the drawbacks of rigid flexibility.

A sensitive and sensible use of the two guidelines of vigilant over-sight and flexible rigidity will provide you with ample supervisory control, while at the same time providing your subordinates with maximum opportunity to produce, learn, grow, and develop.

63

CHAPS ARE AS IMPORTANT AS CHARTS

It's a common pastime of managers, particularly those new in a po-sition, to reshape the organization chart. The basic philosophy of or-ganizing might be changed; span of control widened or narrowed; reporting levels increased or decreased; units (and thus boxes on the chart) added, deleted, or merged; dotted lines and dotted boxes added or deleted. It is certainly valuable to look at the organization of a company, division, or unit every few years and when significant changes are taking place. Times, missions, resources, competitive climate, and functions change, and the organization's chart should attempt to portray as accurately as possible what actually exists, rather than what used to be or what one hopes for.

Organization structure and reporting relations are important to the success of any organization. However, we sometimes overempha-size the attention given to and the importance of the "best" structure and organization charts. Various principles of organizing a company are valuable (for instance, group similar functions, unity of com-mand, span of control), but they must, at times, be taken with several grains of salt.

The point is, beyond the boxes, levels, and lines, it is the people who count. The issue, then, is not the right chart, but as the British would say, the right chap. You want to build your organization on sound principles that are reality-based in terms of the missions, needs, and climate of the organization and the industry. But, above all, you should be concerned about getting and keeping the best people you can at all levels and creating a structure that encourages and allows them to flourish. You may have to violate or modify some organizational principles because of the particular talents, personalities, and operating styles of your most valuable staff. But, if you do so, you want to take into account the effect on the rest of the organization.

For example, though sound organizational principles usually say that you should not have more than 5, 7, 10, or 12 subordinates reporting to one superior (the span of control principle), you may have to modify that. It depends on the capabilities, needs, and style of the superior; ambition of subordinates; rate of change in and on the organization; type, size, and complexity of the organization and industry; communication and delegation techniques used; frequency of contact needed with subordinates, and so forth.

In essence, the basic question is, Does the proposed organization help or hinder good people in accomplishing the organization's goals effectively, efficiently, and economically?

64

FIGHTING THE BATTLE OF THE BUDGET

The annual battle of the budget comes upon us, and each year, given the financial constraints most organizations face, the battle is longer, tougher, and more devastating to the participants and to their continuing relationships.

The budget of a unit or company is a critical management document since it serves as a statement of intent, an operating plan, and a control tool. Budgetary processes, issues, and problems are indeed of critical importance and seriousness in dealing with organizational plans and operations for the next year and the years ahead. However, it may be helpful in terms of at least momentarily relieving tension while at the same time providing useful information to take a slightly less serious look at budgetary tactics used by budget requesters. The budgeting process and decisions are of great importance to individuals, units, and the company as a whole. For many individuals, the scope of their unit's budget determines their prestige, power, title, compensation, and potential within the organization and their attractiveness to other companies. The individual's success in getting budgetary approval for salaries, new staff, space, products, equipment, and so on, enhances his or her own self-image, his or her reputation with others, and morale within the unit.

To assist you in waging the battle of the budget, I offer some techniques or strategies you might employ as a requester to maximize the funds made available to you. I then look at the budget request through the eyes of the reviewer or approver whose goal is to make the least funds available while still accomplishing major objectives.

APPROACHES AND TACTICS FOR THOSE REQUESTING FUNDS

The Duck Hunter. The Duck Hunter uses decoys. You may put in either a very complex or very far-out project or an expensive request, fight hard for it, and then give up with great reluctance. Meanwhile, the reviewer may not have the time or energy to look carefully at your other requests.

The Gardener. In anticipation of pruning during budgeting, sprinkle your requests with lots of water (fat), backed up by slides and graphs, so that after the pruning, you are left with most, all, or some extra over what you really need.

The Savior. "I am not only saving my unit, but also the company if you provide the funds I need."

The Entrepreneur. "If you provide venture capital to meet the targets of opportunity available, I can provide the greatest return on investment in the company's history."

The Fundamentalist. "My department is fundamental to everything that goes on in this company. You cannot call yourself a progressive, healthy organization without a strong unit/function/department. Therefore, I must be supported adequately even if you have to reduce less essential departments."

The Drowning Person. Present impressive evidence of how much you have been underfunded in the past in comparison to your needs and other units. Your plea to the budget makers is to save the drowning man—"Throw us a life preserver and provide the necessary funds."

The Critical Mass Believer. You indicate that if you are to achieve excellence in the particular area you need a critical (larger) mass of staff, equipment, space, discretionary funds, and general funding. You provide data on your calculations as to what constitutes a critical mass, comparisons with other units and organizations, and results to be expected in what time frame.

The Surgeon. Indicate in great detail the cuts you have made into the fat and then into the bone and the blood that has been spilled, as well as the psychological damage done. Then simply say you cannot be responsible for failure to meet unit objectives (they will be almost impossible to meet now) if further cuts are made.

The Gambler. "I've done all that I can in paring my budget. My past track record proves that I produce much on minimum resources. Cut me any further and I cannot be held responsible for failure to accomplish my primary objectives. Also, if you decide to cut, I shall go to the president" (or if you're talking to the president, you can threaten to resign—be careful, your bluff may be called).

The Analyst. You present data in regard to past, present, and future funding and results achieved or to be achieved and compare your unit to others in the company and in competitive companies. Statistics, quantitative measures, graphs, and charts are presented on paper and slides in order to overwhelm the budget makers with the time and thought that have gone into the analysis in providing beyond a shadow of a doubt that your request is fair and reasonable.

The Good Soldier. "I've done the best I can and, as you know, I've always delivered reasonable cuts and good performance. I've followed your requests for a bare minimum budget. I can't do any better; I recommend you make no further cuts. However, if you decide to cut further, I will carry on as best I can."

The Martyr. "If you need a few thousand more, I'll give up my salary increase or the assistant I desperately need." Be careful, the budget maker may take the challenge.

Honest Guy. This is a relatively rare but recommended approach. Play it straight; don't pad; be low key in describing past accomplishments and the unit's problems and concerns. In doing so, you can honestly say there's no fat in your budget. There is, of course, a risk that the budget maker won't believe you and by being cut you will turn into a drowning man.

Play on the Heartstrings. "This is my chance to make my mark . . . my last big chance . . . my last big challenge before I retire . . . I retire in the next two years, I want to go out riding high."

Some Other Approaches. These can best be described in the basic sentence to be used. "Just be fair." "All we want is our fair share based on our performance." "Correct past injustices." "Let's work together on this to lessen the damage; I can help you, you can help me."

APPROACHES AND TACTICS BY THOSE REVIEWING REQUESTS

Suggest a Trade. Offer funding for certain projects or requests in exchange for significant reductions or elimination of other requests.

Be the Devil. If you sense that the requester realizes that you have discovered the fat in his or her budget and is just trying to save face, offer to write a strong memo that will take the requester off the hook. He or she will be able then to call you an S.O.B. and tell his or her staff that he or she was lucky to save their jobs. (Be careful, you don't want to be known as an S.O.B. too often or too widely—use this in extremis.)

Split the Difference. Once you've knocked out as many things as you can based on the strength of your analysis or weakness in the requester's position, offer to split the difference.

Save Time. "Let's save time and anguish. What's your bottom, bottom line? Let's get this over with as quickly as possible."

Conduct an Audit. Scrutinize every detail, develop your own data, put the requester on the defensive, and make him or her appreciate that you are being very soft when you cut out only *X* percent.

The Salesperson. Offer to reshape and improve the budget request and support it strongly to higher authority, while saying you need to have some reductions in the bottom line.

Wait Till Next Year. "You have a reasonable proposal, but I just can't meet your needs this year. Help me out; take *X* percent less this year and I promise you will be in the top priority category next year."

The Honest Guy. Rare, but recommended. Play it straight. Indicate what you have to achieve in reductions and why. Be willing to change your view in light of facts presented.

We have discussed strategies, tactics, and ploys. In one form or another with more or less documentation, sincerity, and vehemence, they will be utilized by one or both of the parties involved in negotiating the budget. The point I conclude with is that despite the game-playing suggested here, we must strive to build budgetary processes that are rational, responsive to the needs of all involved, and based on credibility and integrity. In my own experiences, as both requester and reviewer, I have found that one form or another of the Honest Guy approach pays off—certainly in the long run, but frequently in the short run. This calls for integrity and a lack of gamesmanship on both sides of the table.

65

CONTROL, BUT DON'T OVERCONTROL

Control is an important aspect of management and is related to several other management functions such as planning and budgeting. In fact, in every management function and area you need various levels of control. In an ideal world, everything would go as planned and as set forth in policies and procedures. In the real world, the actions or inactions of individuals and units, the efforts of competitors, internal forces in the organization, and external forces acting on them may make it impossible or very difficult to carry out well-designed plans and procedures.

Controls seek to ensure that results conform to established objectives. To be effective, a control system involves:

1. Establishing performance standards with sufficient specificity so that actual results can be measured against them.
2. Monitoring and measuring performance and comparing the verified results with the standards previously established.
3. Taking action to correct deviations from the standards set and the planned objectives.

It would be easy to set up a very tight system of controls. However, one must evaluate the control system in terms of whether it is cost-effective: Are you spending $100,000 on controls to prevent possible fraud totaling $1,000? Are the controls so burdensome and picayune that they slow up the accomplishment of your objective, damage morale and incentive, harm relations with customers and suppliers, and so on? In essence, you want effective controls that are logical and simple to understand, are flexible and responsive enough to adapt to changing circumstances, are focused on exceptions to the expected, are at critical points for evaluation, and are tuned in to the organization's structure, style, and needs. No control system will work unless there is effective leadership and a reporting system that is objective, accurate, and timely and reaches the right people at the right time so that the information is useful and timely, and corrective action can be taken.

The effective manager will balance the need for control systems and reports with an understanding that people may lack knowledge of or disagree with the performance objectives, the standards and measurements, or the control system's goals. This can be overcome or ameliorated by discussion with those involved and, if possible, agreement as to goals and controls.

An effective control system requires more than a controller's traditional green eyeshade approach or the latest and most powerful information technology and monitoring devices. The carefully designed and discussed control system can accomplish the goals required of such systems while bringing a bonus to management and the organization not usually associated with controls. That bonus is the demonstration that there is a sensitivity and concern for creativity, flexibility, and the motivation and satisfaction of those affected by what is established as a control system and the discussion and communication process involved in design, implementation, and evaluation of the system. Furthermore, such an approach would indicate a commitment to the need for communication and cooperation in achieving the organization's objectives.

66

INNOVATE OR VEGETATE!

Individuals, units, organizations, industries, and society as a whole are concerned about increasing productivity, meeting or beating the competition, and meeting short- and long-term objectives. More capital investment, refurbishment of plant, greater involvement of workers, less restrictive governmental regulations, an emphasis on the work ethic, greater use of technology, and better education and training from grade school on are some of the answers being given to meeting those concerns. A major factor in restoring and maintaining the economic health of the nation will be increased stress on the need for innovation and creation of a climate within organizations that is conducive to innovation.

Failure to do or make something new or better will lead organizations to drift along and be overcome by conditions and competition. Thus, individuals and organizations need to focus on innovation. Innovative thinking is not necessarily essentially deductive or inductive. Innovators can take apparently unrelated items, problems, or opportunities and establish a relationship between them. Innovative organizations don't assume that innovation necessarily flows from greater knowledge about an issue, or from highly educated persons (educational institutions often stifle the creative impulse), or from particular positions or levels within an organization. Creativity and ingenuity can come from research, but they can also come from inspiration, hunches, and the assumption that something can work though conventional wisdom says it can't.

An organization can seek to create a climate for creativity by eliminating or modifying various existing barriers. This involves looking at existing policies, procedures, and controls. These may work to inhibit individualism and departures from the standard or company way of thinking or doing things and, thus, should be modified to encourage deviations from set patterns. Company organization and style of management may inhibit innovation by overcentralizing planning, research, and decision making and by overemphasizing group or committee thinking and specialization versus individual effort. Budgetary processes may be an inhibiting factor in that they require detailed cost justifications, when these may not be possible in exploring a new idea, or by not providing flexibility in meeting new opportunities, challenges, or the development of new ideas that pop up after the budget has been locked in. The appraisal, reward, and recognition system may not give sufficient credit for creative thinking, either in regard to new ideas or for suggestions for improvements by an individual concerning his or her current responsibilities. Too often, the person who finds a way to do what he or she does more efficiently or economically is not amply rewarded because it's considered part of the job, or the manager is not lauded and rewarded for innovations he or she has introduced because "that's what we're paying you for." We should include as an important part of the periodic evaluation and salary review the manager's role in encouraging or bringing about innovations and creative ideas on his or her own part or by subordinates.

It is important to overcome these obstacles by encouraging individuals and units through an appropriate award and recognition system, even if the idea fails, and by providing separate innovation funds for trying different approaches both at the unit level under the control of managers and at higher levels within the organization. A climate should be developed that emphasizes asking questions and exploring ideas about why we do things this way and why not think and try doing it another way? What are our strengths and weaknesses? What are our targets of opportunity now and in the future? What's the future likely to be for our company, industry, and nation, and how can we position ourselves with new or better products or services?

Some techniques can be helpful in unleashing the creative impulses (that may be latent) that many individuals have. These include brainstorming, a review and innovation retreat, analyzing what others do, quality circle approaches, suggestion systems, providing free time (sabbatical) from one's normal duties to focus on new ideas, various team approaches, and working with consultants. It may be helpful for you to think of describing to a very bright, inquisitive person who knows nothing about your area what you and your unit do. Whether you find such a person and try the approach literally or imagine it in a figurative way, you can assume there would be many naive, uninformed, and simplistic questions or suggestions, but these may spark your thinking. Or, you may want to assume that your company has just filed for bankruptcy (or your job or unit was abolished) and you are now trying to start all over. What would be your goals, objectives, policies, procedures, organization, products, services, and so forth? The point is, why not start now before you're bankrupt? Another approach is to imagine that you are dying and you are instructing your next-in-command how he or she should carry on and improve things or you are telling him or her what you always wanted to tell your supervisor, the president of the company, or the board of directors. After you list these things, why not start doing something about them now?

The pressures of the tried and true and the status quo are great indeed. We tend to wait until the "right" time or a crisis comes along to seek new and different ways to think and act. But time, momentum, competition, or calamity may overcome us, and so it is imperative to be constantly seeking to innovate.

67

DECIDE, DAMN IT!

Too often it takes too long to decide on major or even minor actions. It may be that the individual decision maker or the organization itself is afraid to decide or has a style of procrastinating, avoiding decisions, and shifting the buck. Some people are afraid of the risks of any decisive action and so are tempted to see whether the issue will go away, or is not as serious as it seems, or if someone else can stick his or her neck out. Other techniques for decision delay or avoidance include appointing committees, task forces, or a Blue Ribbon Study Commission and employing outside experts.

Certainly, decisions deserve careful study, marshalling of facts, and weighing alternatives, but, after all is said and done, he (or she) who hesitates too long will be lost. Events or competition may overtake you, and a late excellent decision may be no better than an early or on-time good decision.

You have to encourage in yourself and your subordinates—and as a skill and style for all levels in the organization—a sense of a commitment to decisive decision making, an eagerness to decide rather than to avoid making decisions. Being eager does not mean you need jump too quickly or act without thorough analysis. It connotes a sense of satisfaction and resoluteness in being willing to step up to the tough issues that have to be decided, and, based on one's best knowledge, judgment, experience, information, and even intuition, to choose the course of action. It may be that you will decide not to act in a given situation, but that should be a positive judgment not to do something rather than just to let something slide by so that you fail to act by default rather than by decision.

There are risks, of course, in being decisive, but it is far better in today's national and international competitive environment to be willing to take risks and make decisions than to wait until it is crystal clear what course of action should be taken and until complete consensus is reached based on 99.99 percent of the information you can possibly get.

The eight basic steps in decision making are:

1. Recognize that a problem or need for a decision exists.
2. Define the problem or need as clearly and as specifically as possible.
3. Analyze the reasons for and results of the problem or decision situation.
4. Develop and find the most promising alternative solutions or courses of action.
5. Analyze and evaluate the feasible alternatives including a concern for probable and possible positive and negative consequences.
6. Select the best solution or course of action.
7. Implement the solution chosen based on careful planning.
8. Monitor and evaluate results.

In looking at alternatives, always keep in mind how the decision ties in to major goals, what the effects on people will be, what the impact on the organization structure will be, and what the interrelationship is with other decisions.

Decision making is tough, yet exhilarating. The person who steps into the decision maker's batter's box confidently, challenges the pitcher, and takes the best swing is more likely to get the extra base hit than the person who is not confident, prone to be overpowered, and simply seeks to not look bad. In the end, the ultimate test of an executive is his or her judgment and ability as indicated in the decisions he or she makes, and how he or she makes, implements, evaluates, and fine-tunes or changes them

68

NOT ALL DATA ARE INFORMATION, NOT ALL INFORMATION COMES FROM DATA, NOT ALL DATA OR INFORMATION ARE IMPORTANT

As managers, companies, and as a society, we have become information junkies. We want more data, faster, in color, on terminals, with graphics. We want to know more, see more, receive and transmit more, have big machines do it, have our desktop and home computers do it, have telephone lines and cable lines do it. Basically, we believe, as we should, that better decisions and actions come from the knowledge at our command. Thus, what better way to get that knowledge and achieve breakthroughs and competitive advantage than to get all the information (perceived as knowledge) we can, accurately, rapidly, and in a usable form for decision making.

This approach is generally valid, except that you can go overboard. Reams of statistics, hourly or daily reports, automatic monitoring and reporting, all provide data. The important question is, however, are the data useful in providing information for the purposes you need? It is nice to have a lot of data. It makes you feel secure in the event a question is asked, a report is requested, a problem arises. But you should be asking, Who is going to use this, for what purpose, when, how often, and do other ways of getting the data already exist or can they be changed slightly to provide what is necessary? Data are gathered at a cost, even though it may seem very small in comparison to the reams of paper generated.

You have to decide whether the benefits are worth the time and cost involved in generating the data, transmitting them, and reviewing them. All too often, at one point in time, an official has asked for some information, and a considerable amount of work was necessary to answer it. Subordinates then decide to prepare a report on a regular basis so that questions or related questions can be answered almost instantly. But the question may have been a whim or a one-time occurrence, and the automatically generated reports for the next "x" number of years have no value! The computer allows us to do much more, much more quickly, but the question always should be, Is this necessary? People still have to read what the computer has generated—why take their time unless it's necessary, and why use storage space for filing unnecessary reports? Data are useful in various forms, but only when they provide information that is of value to you. What you need, in what form, how often, and with what degree of detail, accuracy, and speed should be carefully thought through before you set in motion computer and manual actions to generate data.

At the same time, we must be aware that not all information comes from reports, database searches, or statistics. Your daily newspaper, business and general publications, seminars, conferences, courses, dinner-party and lunch conversations, your sensitivity, your eyes, ears, and nose, all may provide clues and information that are helpful to you in understanding and acting on problems and opportunities. Thus, you have to be open to ideas, suggestions, and perceptions from a variety of sources to get a well-rounded picture of what's going on.

After all is said and done, if you see yourself as in the center of a whirlpool with all types of data and information being drawn to that center, you must question whether you need to have all of that coming toward you and at you. Given the time and attention span of individuals at various levels in the organization, the organization and the individuals have to be very clear as to what they really do need to know, what is useful to know, what is merely nice to know, and what is not important for them to know unless there is a deviation from the normal or from a plan. With these as general guidelines, you can differentiate among various levels of information needs and eliminate some data and information collection, review, transmission, and storage altogether, and you can refine the list of who should see what, in what form, and how often, thereby saving copies, computer time, and review time by various individuals. You have to be aggressive about getting the information you need, but you also have to be aggressive about the tendency to generate wave after wave of data and information that are not necessary or even useful. Unless we become more aggressive about insisting on getting what's needed and no more, our brains, attention span, computer storage, and retrieval systems will become too clogged up to deal with the really necessary information.

69

GARBAGE IN/GARBAGE OUT AND GARBAGE IN/GOD OUT

The computer age is upon us, so much so that children under ten are learning to program various personal and home computers. Computer literacy is a necessity not only for the college student but also for managers at all levels. But there are fears of the new and the unknown, concern about whether one has the intelligence to learn computing, particularly when recent college graduates (if not teenagers) seem to attack the computer with such ease and confidence. The language is strange (input, output, thruput, bits, bytes, and so on), and the results are somewhat magical. And, beyond all this is the concern that computer hardware, software, and technicians will replace many middle managers, since many middle management jobs constitute compiling, formatting, analyzing, and distributing various kinds of data. A good computer program and, in fact, existing off-the-shelf packages can do more quickly, thoroughly, and accurately what some middle managers do. Thus, the computer poses not only a challenge and opportunity but also a threat to traditional ways of doing things, to power and prestige, and even to the maintenance of one's job.

As we come to rely on computers for much more than just a giant accounting machine, we must be wary of placing too much confidence in them. The machine itself is highly accurate and reliable, but the programs written for it may, in a very few instances, exhibit inaccuracy, lack of thoroughness, or, with a bit more frequency, a lack of responsiveness to the real needs of the user. Although the systems analyst and programmer may be technically proficient, they can make mistakes or have an inadequate understanding of the use to which the data will be put or the scope and the variances of the problem that has led someone in authority to suggest "computerizing" the report or having a Computer Center look at the problem. Whereas in the past there was a trend toward one large computer center serving all units with terminals and access for particular users, now there generally are various centers. In fact, with micro- and minicomputers, personal and home computers, there will be many more hands on the keyboard, including the hands of those who directly need the information.

But as we become more computer dependent and knowledgeable, we must also recognize the limits to computerization, when systems are cost-effective and when they are not. We should also recognize that analysts and programmers are fallible, make mistakes, take the wrong roads, and sometimes view the problem from their perspective as technicians rather than from our perspectives as clients. Thus, even more than ever, the old term GIGO is relevant—Garbage In/Garbage Out. If what has been programmed to meet your needs is basically garbage, that's what will come out of the machine, even though it is on computer paper or appears on a terminal with color graphics. It is also true that we still fall prey to believing that once something has been "computerized" our problem is solved. In essence, the corollary of GIGO is something we must be aware of— Garbage In/God Out.

The successful manager of today and tomorrow will not necessarily be skilled at systems analysis or programming, but he or she will have a basic computer literacy and understanding of the possible applications of computerization and of the approaches and techniques of computer technicians.

The manager and his or her company will understand that the proper use of computers will enable the professional and the manager at all levels to increase productivity and to increase the quantity and scope of responsibilities that can be handled by an individual. With more information available almost instantly, decisions can be made more quickly and with greater precision and with an ability to quickly evaluate alternative courses of action.

The manager must be oriented toward looking for possible computer applications in order to improve productivity, effectiveness, and efficiency. He or she will be wary of GIGO and will understand clearly that computers assist the manager in providing information and in analyzing alternative actions, but they are simply a high-powered technique or tool. They are generally cost-effective, but there have been many instances of massive waste of dollars and time because of poor planning, conceptualization of the problem and solution, implementation, selection and design of hardware, software development, and related problems. Computers in all forms and applications enhance intelligence; they don't replace it.

70

MAKE SURE YOUR BASE IS SOLID BEFORE EXPANDING IT

It is natural for high achievers and those who are successful or who desire success to keep seeking greater challenges and higher mountains to climb. In your drive for greater responsibilities, power, prestige, recognition, and wealth, you look for ways to expand your turf, power, and knowledge. This may come about by seeking to expand your unit's scope of responsibilities, by merging with other units, or by taking over related or entirely separate areas. Success in bringing about increased responsibilities and in managing your expanded base marks you as a person destined for even greater things.

Although the desires outlined are admirable, you have to be careful. Just as companies can expand too rapidly or acquire businesses that require skills different from what they've been successful at, thus leading to failure, the same can be true of the individual executive. In your lust for increased power and responsibility, you may be biting off more than you can chew. You may simply not have the time, resources, or skill to manage as much as you thought you could, at least at this point in your career or at this point in the life of the organization. While you may be up to the challenge of much more and tougher things to do, your staff may not be or may not be willing to work so much harder or longer, and you may not be able to hire more or better staff.

In deciding to make your move for more power, aside from developing strategy and tactics to accomplish that goal, you must also evaluate how solid your base is. In other words, you may be seeking to add additional floors to your house (job responsibilities), but the house may not be built for additional loads or the foundation may not be strong enough.

The danger is that as you get a larger, tougher turf and spend more time on the new and less on the old, the old begins to crumble. You then have to rush to shore up the foundation, and the new begins to crumble, and you end up rushing back and forth, leading rather quickly to disaster for the unit and for you. So before you make your move, check your basic responsibilities. Are you sufficiently in command and on top of the people and systems so that they are in place, enabling things to continue to run smoothly? Is your knowledge base of your area broad and deep enough so that you can very quickly grasp the issues and make decisions, since you will have less time and energy to spend? Are there a sufficient number of good people in your old area so that if you use several in your new areas, quality of effort can still be maintained?

You then have to look to the new areas that you want to take over. Evaluate objectively how good the people and systems are in those areas and whether you will have sufficient time to learn the areas, to climb that learning curve. If you don't have the quality and number of people you need and can't get them, be careful—you may be swallowing something that will cause you to choke. Find out what you don't know and how you can go about filling the gaps in your knowledge. Check whether you have the time, in the face of the needs of the unit, to fill the gap. Even more fundamental, do you have the desire to learn the nitty-gritty of a new area and to deal with the major issues as well as with the mundane, the tough as well as the trivial? It is exciting to tackle new challenges and have more prestige and power, but you have to be realistic and introspective as to whether this is really what you want. Also, can you truthfully handle the new responsibilities now or very soon? Beware of the risk of reaching too far beyond your grasp, too fast, thereby ruining a fine reputation and future.

71

THE PAT ANSWER FOR SUCCESS— PLANNING, ACCURACY, THOROUGHNESS

There are many characteristics and attributes that can be used to describe those who are successful in all organizations. Among those traits that are frequently cited and that led to the formulation of the PAT idea are devotion to and success in Planning, a zeal for Accuracy, and a commitment to Thoroughness.

PLANNING

It is obvious to almost everyone that planning is necessary before one undertakes performing any other management function, such as organizing; obtaining financial, human, and physical resources; staffing; deciding; budgeting; innovating; communicating; representing; controlling; or directing. You have to know what your goals and objectives are before you begin to work out ways to achieve them and you have to plan in regard to each of the management functions.

However, all too frequently not enough time, thought, and full communication with others (those involved and those affected) go into the planning process. Planning is fundamental; it is worth considerable time and effort. However, you must be aware of "paralysis caused by analysis." You can keep on so long searching for more and more information, alternatives, and assessments of risks that you never reach a point of decision or, by the time you do, time and/or competitors have passed you by.

It is important to recognize that two broad categories of factors are involved in planning: the internal factors of an organization and factors external to the organization.

The internal factors include:

1. The organization's history and traditions, past actions, successes, and failures.

2. Managerial and operating style, reward, and motivational structure; how the organization deals with success and failure; how the organization responds to risks and opportunities.

3. Capabilities of present staff and ability to recruit and retain high quality personnel.

4. Mood, momentum, and morale in the organization.

5. Quality and quantity of resources, skills, and technology available in the organization and the quality, quantity, and cost-effectiveness of the products and services it renders or produces.

6. The organization's assets: financial, human, material.

The external factors include:

1. The organization's reputation: local, regional, and national, with its various "constituencies"—customers, clients, suppliers, stockholders, investment firms, governmental agencies, and the general public.

2. Susceptibility to change—in the economy and consumer taste.

3. The impact of past, present, and probable governmental actions, political and economic policy and values, international political and economic conditions and climate.

4. The impact of actions by competitors or potential competitors.

5. Dependability and reliability of governmental and other services—mail, telephone, utilities, railroads, and so on.

6. Demographic trends in regard to customers, the labor force, and society in general.

7. The impact of technology, the availability and cost of money and capital goods, the availability and price of natural resources, raw and manufactured materials.

8. The impact of psychological and societal factors—definition of the good life, individuals' aspirations, and optimism or pessimism about the present and future.

What you should focus on in developing any plan is its contribution to accomplishing your objectives, that it is regarded as a critical function by managers at all levels, that possible adverse consequences and the efficiency of plans are analyzed, and that the planning premises must be accepted and be consistent throughout the organization. You must also recognize the difficulties in planning: the resistance to change and the questioning of basic premises; the heavy investments, personal, financial, and material that may have already been made in capital equipment, machinery, processes, advertising, products, and people; and the considerable time and expense involved in proper planning. Despite all that is involved, a commitment to planning throughout the organization is vital if you are to increase your chances for success in reaching your goals and, to some measure, controlling your fate.

ACCURACY

Approximations, guesstimates, and rounding off are fine, sometimes, but usually at higher levels and for general purposes. What is important is that a major criterion for evaluating individuals and units is the accuracy in the numbers and data they present, the research and analysis they do, and the quality (accuracy) of the product or service they produce. From the very beginning of a person's employment, the stress should be on the fact that the work presented should not be approximately correct, but 100 percent correct, within the constraints of time and resources available and the cost and benefits of striving for total accuracy. Of course, there will be errors and products that don't pass quality control, or are caught at the last moment, or are discovered later, sometimes at considerable cost and embarrassment. While you should recognize that perfection is highly unlikely and highly costly, it is critical that throughout the organization there be a drive for coming as close to it as possible. Managers have to depend on the validity and accuracy of the numbers, or of research and analysis presented to them; otherwise, they will have to spend their time "checking the numbers." That's a considerable, unnecessary expense. Managers and top executives should be evaluating the premises and assumptions, the alternative approaches, and positive and negative consequences. But all of that is based on the accuracy of the material presented to them. Thus, at lower levels various checking and control systems can be set up on a cost-effective basis to ensure accuracy.

THOROUGHNESS

Linked to accuracy and planning is the concept of thoroughness. Again, from the beginning of your employment and throughout the organization there should be a stress on thoroughness in work effort. Top management should be assured that in the proposed actions being recommended to them, various alternatives have been considered; cost and benefits have been evaluated; various bases and information sources within and outside the organization have been touched and tapped; negative and positive consequences have been taken into account; internal and external environment factors have been calculated; impact on short- and long-term goals, people, reputation, and resources have been carefully analyzed; full-scale implementation and contingency plans have been put in place; and so forth. Good management requires that, as much as humanly possible, there has been thoroughness in all aspects of the work effort. Of course, one must weigh what the costs in dollars, time, and competitive disadvantage might be in being "too thorough," but, generally, the larger the decision, problem, or project, or the more important the results are to the organization's health or profit, the more thorough you want to be.

There's much more to successful management than the PAT answer given, but it does offer a good foundation.

72

DON'T SQUANDER YOUR MOST IMPORTANT PERSONAL RESOURCES— TIME, ENERGY, THOUGHT

Your most valuable personal resources are your time, energy, and thought, and you should do all that you can to protect yourself from wasting them.

Much has been written about time management. I would like to suggest that just as in dieting, some plans are better than others, and it is very easy to discard or modify the plan and put on weight (waste time) again. Willpower and concern are the most important factors in success. Therefore, in regard to managing your time you might begin by maintaining a log over a typical week or two to see what you are spending your time on. Then decide what's important and what's not and ask whether you are allocating your time appropriately and how can you make the necessary changes. Recognize that the usual time wasters are:

Telephone. Too many calls, too-long calls, difficulty in placing calls. *Possible solutions:* Have calls screened, prepare notes for telephone conversations and ask your subordinates to do so when calling you, avoid interruptions by setting aside a time to make and return calls.

Visitors. Too many drop-in or unsolicited visitors. *Possible solutions:* Screening, making clear you prefer scheduled appointments. Essentially, you can save time by not fragmenting it, while recognizing that emergencies or rank will always cause some unscheduled visitors or make it necessary for you to visit someone else.

Meetings. Too many, too long-lasting. *Possible solutions:* Review whether each meeting is necessary, how frequently meetings should occur, who should be there, how long they should be. Also, use agendas, distribute workpapers in advance, make clear what the goals of the meeting are, keep on schedule.

Reading. Too many memos, journals, reports to read. *Possible solutions:* Decide what's important for you to see and eliminate the rest, suggest improvements in writing format and style so that reports and memos are more concise.

Poor Delegation. Work not delegated to others or you spend too much time checking on what they have done. *Possible solution:* You may have to change your management style to allow others to grow, and learn, and have more responsibility.

Poor Scheduling. Your time is committed to appointments, meetings, lunches, dinners, and returning phone calls that are not important or necessary. *Possible solution:* Be strict with yourself and provide clear guidelines to your secretary as to how and with whom to slot your time. When in doubt, you should be consulted.

I believe that most people, in following the preceding, can pick up 1 to 2 hours a day (or more)—a very significant increase in productivity—that could be used for more important aspects of their job and for planning and thinking, thus increasing productivity, performance, and job satisfaction for themselves and their organizations. To accomplish this will require constant vigil and a stress on being clear about objectives and results to be achieved, eliminating and delegating work, and avoidance of overscheduling your time, so that from one third to one half of your time is available for thinking, planning, crises, and interruptions.

Your two other most valuable resources are energy and thought. Both require you to be in as good condition as you can be—physically, mentally, emotionally, and psychologically. Thus, you should show reasonable concern about checking your health, the need for regular exercise (it has physical as well as nonphysical benefits), your diet, and your drinking, smoking, and drug use. You also should look at your nonwork time in terms of best utilizing the satisfactions and change from work life that they provide. On the job you should be concerned about having the time and opportunities to utilize and channel your energy and thoughts in a way that produces maximum effectiveness and satisfaction. You should be concerned that you use your energy, thinking capacity, and time on matters of significant importance. Don't waste them on inconsequential matters.

Perhaps the biggest obstacle to effective use of energy and thought is the presence of stress and tension. Thus, you should be concerned about dealing with and overcoming stress as far as you can. A reasonable amount of stress can get the adrenaline flowing and be of help; an unreasonable amount or an amount you cannot handle can be debilitating.

To meet the stress problem for yourself and others you might:

- Step back and analyze what's causing the stressful situation and what, if anything, you can do to moderate the stress. It may be that the organization or industry is a very stressful one that runs counter to your own desires and style and, thus, is not the organization for you. On the other hand, there may be factors within the organization and the organizational design itself that can be changed to reduce stress.

- Try to develop a work pace that minimizes mental, physical, and emotional strain and fatigue. Try to vary things in regard to pace, challenge, and tempo.

- Use lunch breaks or coffee breaks, when possible, as a means to unwind.

- Try to maintain a balance between your work and nonwork life with a concern for exercise, relaxation, hobbies, and outside interests not related to work.

- Use some type of relaxation exercise on a regular basis and as needed during the work day, for instance, breathing exercises and meditating exercises.

By investing in time and stress management, you can appreciably increase the yield on your most valuable investments and resources—your time, energy, and thought.

73

USE THE RIGHT DOSES OF POWER AND PRESTIGE—MASSIVE FORCE ISN'T NECESSARY, OR KEEP YOUR AUTHORITY IN YOUR HIP POCKET

It is tempting to use the full force of your power, prestige, and authority in order to quickly achieve your goals, prove that you can accomplish things more effectively than others, or just impress yourself and the organization with your ability and power. Those who are experienced in management recognize that such actions, while feeding their ego and perhaps impressing their staff, can lead to serious negative effects and, ultimately, to diminishing their power and prestige.

It is good and important to know what authority, power, and strength you have and the resources, access, poker chips, and IOUs that are available to you in case of need. But, just because you have more strength than those you are dealing or negotiating with, it does not necessarily mean that you have to use it to accomplish your goals. In management, people have a good sense of the pecking order and who really has influence, even if the organization charts and position descriptions don't coincide with reality. When some people speak, endorse, or act, by formal, informal, or reality-based authority, others will listen, agree, and respond positively. The reverse is also true. In spite of rank, a person is often ignored or humored because of lack of authority or influence and because others know that he or she has no real power.

Assuming you indeed have real power, you must ask yourself how much you use in a given situation, why, and how. If you look at your authority, prestige, and power as limited resources rather than unlimited ones, you can then begin to focus on using your resources only when needed, in an amount that accomplishes your objectives without being wasteful, and in a manner, if possible, that does not lead to negative reactions, which would cause you to use more of your precious resources. If persuasion and discussion can lead to the action you want, why use an order? If a mild reminder, suggestion, or even reprimand will lead to the desired corrected action, why use threats or formal written reprimands? If you can bring about changes in performance and attitude without suspending or firing, why not avoid such actions?

Occasionally, you may have to assert your prerogatives just to indicate that they are there and that if called for, you will use the power you have. But this should not be done as a show-off sort of thing, but only if the conditions warrant it and in a manner that does not employ an excessive reaction to a mild problem. Some managers want to demonstrate forcefulness and snuff out any problem by killing it several times over. But just as it does not make sense to use a cannon when a pistol will accomplish your goal, a measured response should be utilized at those times when you need to demonstrate your authority. You don't want to overcommit yourself on trivial issues. If they blow up, you look foolish; and if you invest too much on small things, even though they succeed, you also look foolish. Why put so much on the line for so little? It indicates the wrong priorities, perceptions, and use of your authority. You need not be waving your authority around, referring to it, demonstrating it, wearing it on your sleeve. It is far more effective to keep it buried in your hip pocket, unseen, but easily reachable when necessary.

In short, once you and others know you have authority and power, you don't have to demonstrate it often. It is much better to use these resources rarely, but effectively, and thus, to paraphrase

Teddy Roosevelt, to gain a reputation for speaking and acting softly yet persuasively, while not even showing the big stick, though being able and willing to use it when necessary.

$$74$$

SATISFACTION AND SUCCESS DEPEND ON YOUR ABILITY TO **ROAR**

————— ⬛×⬛ —————

Each of us approaches new and tougher positions and responsibilities with high hopes, great expectations, and pleasant dreams of success and professional and personal satisfaction. Sometimes we find rather quickly or over a period of time that our dreams have become nightmares.

There are a number of factors at work in allowing you to achieve your dreams and avoid nightmares. Many have been discussed elsewhere in this book. As a general approach, I have identified four factors, but the list could easily be tripled. I suggest that if you are able to ROAR, your chances for achieving your goals increase significantly.

Responsibilities. First, you will probably need to have the kind of responsibilities that are challenging and stimulating to you, now, short range, and long range. They should provide an opportunity for growth and learning on your part. They should tap your skills and knowledge and push these to greater heights. They should fit your management style and your personality or at least give you the impetus and incentive to make modifications without making you uncomfortable. Many people seek not only maximum responsibility in depth in an area, but also desire breadth of responsibility. The responsibilities may be exactly what you like, but if the organization is inhospitable, the authority insufficient, and the resources inadequate, your success and satisfaction are highly unlikely or impossible.

Organization. Organization is important in terms of your ability to organize your activities, staff, priorities, and time in a way that you consider effective and efficient. Beyond your own unit, department, or division, you must be concerned about the organization as a whole. Where do you and your unit fit? How important are your responsibilities to the organization? Is there a logical and rational division of responsibilities in the organization or is work and responsibility organized in a way that will hinder decision making, create conflict, and erode effectiveness? Do the organization's priorities, policies, practices, management style, history and tradition, concern for high standards of performance, job and customer satisfaction, climate and environment, and stress on flexibility and creativity help or hinder the achievement of your professional and personal goals? Will you be proud to be part of the organization?

Authority. Your responsibilities and the organization may meet your highest expectations, but it often happens that your authority to achieve your goals is unclear, undefined, or inadequate. The management textbooks often discuss the importance of having authority commensurate with responsibility, but in many organizations this does not occur. In essence, to succeed you need to have the ability, influence, and clout to be able to suggest, convince, cajole, and cooperate with others, and, when necessary, to order others to respond to your needs, ideas, and directions. You will not want to wave the big stick of authority all the time or even frequently, but when you need it, it should be there.

Resources. Finally, you need to have the right quality and quantity of resources in order to be successful. You can be the brightest, most hardworking, creative, charismatic manager and leader in the country, but if, for some reason or another, adequate resources are not available to you in a timely fashion, you are doomed to fail. The less able will fail more quickly, but even the most able manager will fail. Thus, if at all possible, before you undertake new responsibilities you should have a very clear commitment as to what resources will be available to you now, short term, and long term in order to accomplish specific goals. The appropriate resources involve operating and capital funds; quality and quantity of staff with appropriate mechanisms to reward good performance and discipline or terminate poor performance; machinery and equipment, including office equipment and computer hardware and software support; space and facilities; and research and contingency funds.

If you feel comfortable with the answers and expectations as you apply the ROAR factors, the chances are great indeed that you will be able to roar with success.

75

PREPARE YOURSELF FOR THE CLIMB TO SUCCESS

Your management training does not end the day you receive your bachelor's or master's degree. Those who succeed in management are continuously growing and learning. Standing still in regard to acquiring new knowledge and skills and to improving your existing knowledge and skills means that you will soon be overtaken and passed by others and by events.

In essence, the day you begin a job is the time to map out a growth and learning plan for your current job, for what you hope will be your next job, and for the one or two jobs after that. You have to sketch what you think you will have to know now and in the future to do well in the current position and in various positions you hope to hold. This requires an understanding of the responsibilities of the positions and the problems and opportunities you face. If you list responsibilities, activities, and functions of the various positions in one column, you can list in another column the skills, attributes, knowledge, and experience that are necessary. Your third column can be ways in which to acquire what is necessary, your next-to-last column will be a timetable for starting and ending the acquisition of these necessities, and your last column will indicate successful completion, changes, and comments.

For some skills or knowledge, you will need various types of on-the-job experience, for instance, serving on a task force, being a project team director, serving as "assistant to." Other skills can only be acquired by various types of formalized training, such as university courses, company training programs, conferences, professional and training organization courses, community services, and so on. The needs you have or foresee can include training in regard to use of computers, telecommunications, marketing, financial analysis, supervisory techniques, various technical areas, quantitative analysis, economics, governmental regulations, international marketing, foreign languages, budgeting, planning, speed reading, stress management, business communications, and so forth.

Your focus should be on what you need to know now and in the next year or two, but just as important, what you need to know three to five years from now and five to ten years from now. From time to time, evaluate, modify, and update the plan so you're always looking to the future as well as the present. Acquiring the knowledge and experience you need helps you chart your course for future advancement because you will have demonstrated intelligence, foresight, and ambition in developing skills for the future. The progressive company will also be doing manpower planning and advising, and guiding and developing opportunities for those on the fast track to acquire new knowledge and skills. It is helpful for you to discuss with your supervisor and with his or her supervisor as well as with the training department what they see as the needs of the company. Request their advice and assistance in helping you develop skills in these areas.

In effect, your learning and growth plan is your personal development or capital (intellectual and experiential skills) growth plan. Invest significant time in its development and implementation.

76

FIGHT LATENT, COVERT, AND OVERT SEXISM AND RACISM

As a society, the United States has made significant progress over the past three decades in fighting racism and sexism. But despite that progress in employment and almost all areas of society, there is much still to be done.

In most organizations, overt sexism and racism has decreased very sharply in the past two decades, although difficulties in regard to hiring and promotions do come up. You must continue to be vigilant and make clear from the top down to every level that racism and sexism will not be tolerated and that practice of such will result in disciplinary action up to and including termination. In a sense, the problem is now more difficult due to the possibility of latent or covert discrimination. "We would like to hire more blacks and women, but . . . we can't find any qualified people . . . those qualified demand too high a salary or leave us very soon for a better job . . . my people are complaining about reverse discrimination because the blacks/women we've hired aren't as good as people we have turned down or those we've recently hired." Some of the same problems come up in promotions. In both hiring and promotions, white males have a real concern that, though qualified, they are passed over for a black person or a woman who may have scored lower on an examination or had less good performance evaluations or less experience.

The preceding statements could be true or they could be a reflection of latent racism or sexism. The organization committed to providing equal opportunity will attempt to make clear its abhorrence of attitudes, actions, comments, or "jokes" that indicate discriminatory feelings and disrespect. Once the corporate policy, attitude, and actions are known in this area, sexism and racism are likely to be less of a problem. People's prejudices may not be changed by an organization's strong stand, but their actions will be changed if they know that certain things are just not permitted.

Thus, supervisors at various levels can make clear that they want those hiring to actively seek out qualified minorities and women, using the resources of the company, professional associations, and civic, community, minority, and women's organizations. If there are relatively few minorities and women in the company or in higher positions, there may be a company policy that, all other things being reasonably equal, there will be preferential hiring or promotion and that progress will be monitored and considered a criterion in the supervisor's performance evaluation. However, the organization must be concerned about the impact on morale of "reverse discrimination" charges. Organizations may wish to establish special training programs and mentor relationships so that groups of people who have been disadvantaged in one way or another or had access and opportunity blocked, can now, with help, make up for lost time and opportunity. Furthermore, a company can monitor progress of its minority or women employees to see that there is no latent discrimination in regard to good assignments, salary increases, and promotions.

There is another aspect of sexism that is worth noting, and that involves sexual harassment. Again, the organization must make clear in word and action that sexual harassment of women (although there could also be harassment of men) either overt, latent, or through use of "jokes" and innuendo will not be tolerated.

In all of these considerations, a climate and apparatus must be created so that those who feel discriminated against or harassed have a way in which to bring their allegations to the attention of the proper individuals. They should know that they will get a fair hearing, that action will be taken, and that they will not be blamed or hurt if they come forward with their charges.

All organizations need people of talent and dedication. They, and we as a nation, cannot afford to exclude, hamper, or hold back minorities and women who, if given a fair opportunity, could make contributions at least equal to those made by majority-group members and males.

77

QUESTIONS FOR INTERVIEWS

At some point, you will be interviewing individuals to work for you or in your unit.

It is important to recognize that the interview serves to provide information, insights, and perceptions to the interviewer (as well as the interviewees). It is both a screening and decision-making process and tool. It separates qualified from unqualified candidates, outstanding from good and fair candidates. Used correctly, the interview helps the interviewer determine whether:

1. There is the correct "fit" between the candidate and the position.

2. His or her personality will mesh with the rest of the management team.

3. His or her experience, training, past accomplishments, personal goals, management style, and concerns meet and match with the company's present and future needs.

4. His or her communications ability, thought processes, manner, confidence, appearance, creativity, drive, maturity, enthusiasm, broadness of view, sensitivity and concern for results, problem-solving ability, interpersonal relations, aspirations, and performance expectations for himself or herself and others meet the company's present and future needs.

5. There is considerable potential and desire for growth and learning on the part of the individual so that he or she will be able to shoulder additional responsibilities in a few years and whether the individual has the potential to be a major official in the company.

The interviewer's questions must explore viewpoints as well as experience; they must be as tough as the problems that will face the individual who gets the job. The interviewer must be able to hear what the candidate is saying, and what the candidate fails to say. The interviewer must be tuned in to the content as well as the tone and style of the responses.

The interviewer must remember that candidates are trying to make a good impression. They're trying to demonstrate their perceptiveness, clarity of thought, analytical ability, high standards of performance, and aspirations.

It is also important to remember that the interviewer should provide the prospective candidate with the information he or she needs in order to determine whether this job is the one the candidate really wants and will do well at. In a sense, the candidate is selling himself or herself, but the interviewer is also selling the company and the particular position.

There are many specific questions that can be asked to meet the five general concerns cited previously. I have selected 10 key questions that I have found most useful.

Questions

1. What major things have you accomplished in your present position, how were they accomplished, and what were your goals for the next year, two years, three years?

2. What are you proudest of in terms of professional and personal accomplishments throughout your life, and why are these important to you?

3. What would you have liked to accomplish in your present and previous positions that you did not accomplish either in whole or in part, and why were you unable to reach your goals?

4. I assume that at some point in your career you were in head-to-head competition with an individual for a promotion or status or project managership or something of that type. What would an outstanding and fair competitor say about your strengths and weaknesses? What do you regard as your major strengths and weaknesses?

5. What do you think will be the toughest aspects of this job, the most enjoyable aspects, the least enjoyable aspects?

6. What do you think your most significant accomplishments will be in the first year, two years, three years, five years?

7. What are your personal goals in regard to this position, short- and long-term, and in regard to the rest of your career?

8. What criteria would you use in measuring your own perfor- mance in the next and following years and what criteria would you like to have your supervisors use?

9. What criteria and expectations would you use and have in regard to the performance of your subordinates, peers, and supervisor?

10. Why do you want to leave your present position, why do you want this job, why should we hire you?

You might also be prepared for questions that the prospective em- ployee might ask in order to gain information and further his or her candidacy. In fact, if you are a candidate for a new position or pro- motion, you might want to use these questions (and be prepared to answer the previous questions).

Questions. (Compensation matters are not included since they are best left for follow-up interviews after the field has been narrowed down.)

1. The new person will face many specific responsibilities and problems, immediate, short-, and long-term. Which do you re- gard as most important and most difficult?

2. How do you like to deal with a subordinate? How do you handle delegation of responsibility and authority and to what degree, making assignments, regular meetings, dealing with problems, general operating style, characteristics you like and dislike in a subordinate?

3. As you see it, what are the major challenges, opportunities, re- wards, and stimulation of my job and what are the major frustra- tions? What are the major challenges, stimulation, difficulties, and frustrations of your job?

4. What are the strengths and weaknesses of my unit and of my subordinates?

5. What are the responsibilities of those I will work most closely with (peers and those above me) and what are their strengths and weaknesses?

6. What immediate, short- and long-term problems and opportunities exist for your area and the company as a whole? What do you hope to accomplish in the next few years and in the future?

7. What opportunities are there for growth and advancement in my area of responsibility in the company?

8. Why did my predecessor leave the position? What were his or her strengths, weaknesses, accomplishments, failures or, if this is a newly created position, what factors led to the decision that this position should be created?

9. What criteria will you use for my performance evaluations and what objectives do you expect me to accomplish within six months, a year, two to three years, five years? When and how will evaluation be conducted?

10. After 6 months, 1 year, 5 years, 10 years, how will you know you made the right decision in hiring the person for this position? If the position were offered, why should I accept it?

Asking and evaluating the answers to the preceding questions will take considerable time and effort. But for both interviewer and prospective employee, the questions and the answers are important factors in making a critical decision—offering or accepting a position of challenge and responsibility.

78

EVALUATING JOB OFFERS— SAIL THE SEVEN C'S

———— ✳✕✳ ————

If you are successful, you will be approached by companies or executive search firms about changing positions. Or, on your own initiative, as a result of your desire for new or greater opportunities or because you are dissatisfied with or let go from your present job, you will be weighing alternative jobs.

Assuming you have a choice among possible new positions or remaining at your present company versus other offers, by sailing the Seven C's you will be less likely to make an error in your final decision. In order to reach the ideal port of an excellent and satisfying position, the C's to be traveled represent an analysis and evaluation of content, challenge, climate, chemistry, concern, compensation, community.

1. *Content of the Position.* In evaluating the content of a position, you are concerned about the responsibilities and authority of the position, the day-to-day activities, the what-is-to-be-done and how-is-it-to-be-done. You should be interested in understanding in as concrete a fashion as possible short- and long-range objectives, goals, tasks, plans, and opportunities. Imagine what your first month, six months, year, and two years will be like—what issues, problems, or situations are you likely to face and do you have (or will you have) the knowledge, skills, resources, and opportunities to deal with them effectively?

As you look at the position and down the road, you should be asking yourself, Is this the type of position that I would like to hold for a number of years, that trains and positions me for further advancement? What is the status of the position, the power in the position, the ego gratification and self-actualization realizable immediately, short-, and long-term?

You should also be honest with yourself and look at the negative aspects of the position, and there are such aspects to every job. How much trivial work or activity is involved in the position? How much time and effort will be taken up by tasks that involve skills and activities that you regard as unappealing because: (1) they are beneath your knowledge, experience, and position level; (2) they are not interesting; (3) you are not particularly good at them or just don't have the necessary skills and are unable or unwilling to learn them?

2. *Challenge of the Position.* Evaluating challenge in a position involves subjective as well as objective elements based on the position itself, the level of the position, and the needs and attributes of a particular individual. Your age, personality, family circumstances, ambition, experience, lifestyle, managerial style, and work history will all have an influence on how you perceive a particular challenge. You have to be realistic and recognize whether there's too much challenge or whether the tensions and stress connected with the challenge may be more than you want, particularly if the stress is likely to be sustained over a long period.

Some of the questions that should be asked in regard to challenge are as follows: Does the position provide the opportunity to make a significant difference to the success of the unit or the organization as a whole, immediately, short-term, and long-term? Is there enough in the content and climate of the position to keep my brain cells and energy cells going at full power both short- and long-term? Is there enough to keep my ambition, drive, and fire in the belly going full blast? Are the problems real, tough, exciting, and do they provide a sense of accomplishment, self-fulfillment, and self-actualization? Is there a sense of full utilization of particular skills, interests, and abilities? Does the position provide the opportunity to grow, to learn, to expand, to be visible, to be respected and rewarded? Will there be sufficient resources available to get the responsibilities accomplished? Is there sufficient authority to go with the responsibilities? Am I free to make changes in objectives, style, staffing? Does the position meet my personal and family lifestyle and aspirations? Do the demands of the position conflict with how and where I want to live? What is the psychic income of the position? What resources are available to me, directly or indirectly? What is my freedom to change things? How and under what criteria will I be evaluated?

3. *Climate of the Position Itself and within the Organization.* Some positions may pass with flying colors the tests you make in regard to content and challenge; the work environment, however, may pose significant drawbacks. It may be a great job, but in a poor department or in a company that leaves a lot to be desired. You will not be working in isolation and thus what happens around you is important and will have a major impact on how you will operate, whether you will be happy and whether you will succeed or fail. You need to assess the climate and environment of the position, department, and organization.

The following questions can aid you in that assessment: How do my personality, management style, and my technical and managerial skills mesh with supervisors, peers, subordinates, and others in the organization and the organization's history, traditions, and probable future? What is the leadership style of the organization? What are the physical and psychological working conditions in the unit and the organization? What is the climate, tone, and mood of the unit, the organization, and the industry? What challenges does the organization face? What is its reputation? How is the organization doing financially and competitively? Is morale high; is there a sense of esprit de corps? What does the short- and long-term future seem to hold for the organization? What is the prestige, reputation, and past history of this position and this particular unit in the organization and in the field—what does the future seem to hold? How open are communications in the organization? What is the level of competency, performance, motivation, drive, and creativity of supervisors, peers, and subordinates? How high are the standards of performance and how are they being met? Why is there a vacancy? Why are they interested in me? What job security is offered (e.g., a tight employment contract)?

4. *Chemistry.* Of great importance is your sense of how well you will get along with your direct superior. Also of importance is your feeling comfortable with those above you, your peers, colleagues, and subordinates. In essence, the issue is how well do your personality, style, goals, strengths, and weaknesses mesh with your

supervisor's and the others mentioned? Sometimes, given two or three interviews and only two or three hours with the individual, you will have to rely mainly on your gut feeling of whether you like, feel comfortable with, and respect the individual and believe that you will both wear well together.

You should be asking yourself the following: What's my sense of how well I will like working for my supervisor? Will I respect his or her knowledge, ability, reputation, managerial style, personal traits? How do the supervisor's personality, sense of humor, managerial style, and strengths and weaknesses mesh with mine? What does he or she seem to be like as a person and as a supervisor and how does this meet my needs and expectations? What are the supervisor's goals for me and for himself or herself? Does the supervisor seem to be open and honest, concerned about assisting me and helping me develop? Is the supervisor going to call the shots or provide general guidance? Is he or she going to invest time and energy on my problems? How will I communicate with the supervisor and vice versa; how accessible and supportive will he or she be? Will the supervisor back me up when I'm right and be helpful in correcting me when I'm wrong? How will he or she evaluate me? Do I like the supervisor—do I sense an ability to feel close to him or her as a supervisor and person and vice versa? How do all of the preceding factors apply to those on the same level with me with whom I will interact frequently, my subordinates, and others I will interact with frequently?

5. *Concern for Results and People.* You are about to make a commitment to an organization. Your reputation and future, livelihood, and job satisfaction are at stake and, thus, you should be concerned about whether you are, in effect, investing yourself in the right company. Ideally, you should seek an organization that has an outstanding future and strives to be better no matter how good it is now. At the same time, you should be interested in the importance it places on those who work in the company—beyond profits, bottom line, and return on investment.

Some of the questions to be asked are: Is there a concern about achieving ambitious goals, about being good now and constantly getting better whether in terms of profit, market share, quality of service, reputation, and so on? Is there a long-range perspective as well as an emphasis on meeting immediate needs? Is there an equal concern about the people in the organization, their goals, aspirations, learning, growth, compensation, challenges, physical and psychological work environment, psychic income? Is there a concern about job satisfaction at all levels and is there two-way communication?

6. *Compensation.* Up till now you have dealt with basic factors of the job and the environment in your decision-making voyage. You have also been evaluating compensation, but in terms of psychic income rather than monetary income. At different levels and at different stages of your career, monetary compensation will vary in importance. At some points in your career, it may be the paramount factor in selecting a position or in providing job satisfaction. At other points, it may rank fourth, fifth, or even lower in importance to you. No matter where it ranks, you should evaluate the monetary compensation aspects of the position as carefully as other factors, with a concern for net disposable income and impact on your lifestyle and financial security now and in the future.

Questions to be asked are: What are the compensation arrangements for the position and how does it compare with similar levels in the organization, in the field, and with those who, for whatever reasons, I compare myself? How well does the package offered meet my particular concerns for disposable income, base salary, bonus, deferred compensation, employee benefits package, stock options, time off, entertainment and travel allowance, various types of perks, pension, insurance, and early retirement?

How will relocation concerns be handled (taking into account mortgage rates, cost of moving and buying and setting up a new home, tax differences, income tax, real estate, school tax, guaranteeing the sale of present home, need for private schools for children, differences in cost of living, and availability in the company or in the new location of a position for my spouse)? What are reasonable compensation expectations for the short and long range, assuming good or outstanding performance?

7. *Community.* Executives today are much more likely than in the past to turn down positions (or promotions or transfers) that involve relocation. Concern for impact on family, change in lifestyle or climate, and removing oneself from family and friends have a great influence on decision making.

If a relocation is necessary, you should evaluate the new community in which you will live: the quality and type of housing; schools; cultural, recreational, and sports activities and facilities; entertainment; shopping; religious, intellectual, and civic organizations, facilities, and opportunities; public services; transportation; health facilities; taxes; weather; geographic location; housing costs; cost of living; hospitality to newcomers; family and friends located in the area; the nature of the community in terms of values, lifestyle; and so on. Not only the monetary costs of relocation should be considered, but also the impact on the family. If it is important that your spouse have a full or part-time position, what are the opportunities for an appropriate position and advancement opportunities and how can your prospective employer be helpful?

Not every question in each category need apply, nor will every answer be completely satisfactory. However, when making the critical and tough decision involved in choosing a new position, you must take the factors outlined into account. You must carefully consider the facts as you know them, as well as the perceptions and gut feeling you have about the position and the organization. Careful probing, thorough analysis, and objective introspection in regard to the organization and your own abilities, attributes, desires, needs, and goals—immediately, short-, and long-term—will result in a solid and sound basis for reaching a most important decision.

79

THE BOTTOM LINE IS CRITICAL— HOW YOU GOT THERE IS ALSO CRITICAL

There are various measures you can use in regard to assessing the performance of an organization—return on investment, net sales to working capital, current ratio, quick ratio, and so forth. Whether it is a profit or not-for-profit organization, the most essential financial measure is the bottom line on the balance sheet. The questions you can ask if you are to use the bottom line as a management information tool rather than just an accounting record are: Did the organization (or the unit within it) operate at a profit or loss? What caused the bottom line result? How did the result compare against budget and against prior years' performances? Even if it operated at a profit, how did the actual result stack up against what should have been expected in terms of expenses, income, results of comparable units and profit centers in the company, return on investment, direct competitors' results, industry results, and results in the economy as a whole?

The preceding questions provide the first level of analysis of what the numbers on the bottom line really mean. There is another, deeper level of analysis that should be undertaken. Essentially, you need to know how you got to the bottom-line numbers since they may indicate unusual events and actions that are one-time occurrences and, therefore, should not be used as a basis for future projections or planning. Or, they may indicate potential problems and/or opportunities for the next year and/or several years down the road. A company or division, either accidentally or by design, may have sold off inventory and thus looks better than it really is. A competitor may have been on strike and sales were higher than normal. Actions may have been taken that make the bottom line look good for this year, but at the expense of mortgaging or endangering the future. Alternatively, the results may look bad for this year, but the foundation has been laid for excellent results in the future. There may have been some change in accounting philosophy, or practice, or a one-time benefit or harmful event that greatly influenced the final number. Bad or good luck, timing, and economic, political, competitive, or natural events may have a profound impact on the year's results and the outlook for the future.

Whether the numbers on the bottom line look good or bad, the manager of a unit, top executives, and the board of directors need to spend a considerable amount of time analyzing why and how the results are what they are. The focus should be on what facts and lessons are to be learned and what assumptions or changes in planning and operations must be made in order to apply the lessons learned. The joy in your heart about a "great" bottom line can quickly turn to sorrow depending on the analysis of how and why the results were obtained. The sophisticated manager realizes that even more important than the bottom line is how you got there.

80

CHOOSE YOUR PREDECESSORS CAREFULLY

We all know that an important aspect of management is training your possible successors. But before you have to be concerned about training your successors, you have to be in a position to have successors. Thus, one of the criteria in deciding to take a new position in another organization or your current organization is to choose your predecessors carefully.

Before you take on new responsibilities, you should find out as much as you can about your predecessor—his or her strengths, weaknesses, style, accomplishments, and failings. Then look as objectively as possible and evaluate yourself by the same criteria and how you compare with him or her in each area. Ideally, if the person did a poor or unsatisfactory job, your goal would be to have strengths and a style that are better suited to the needs of the organization and that offer a positive contrast. If your predecessor has a good record, your aim is to look for where you can be different and perhaps better and to ascertain that in his or her areas of strength, you are not particularly weak. By doing this matchup, you're better able to judge whether the odds are in your favor of being perceived as at least equal to a very good predecessor and better to significantly better compared with a weak or average one.

If you're lucky, you'll have a predecessor who was fair to poor so that you can make some quick as well as long-range improvements and thus look good not only in terms of ideas, execution, supervision, and so on, but also in terms of style. A poor predecessor can make you look better than you really are! Be careful if you are following a person who was a disaster. Although this gives you the greatest likelihood for some quick victories and opportunities to look outstanding, you may be inheriting a real mess and hidden land mines all along the way. The challenge may be great indeed, but you may not be able to significantly improve the situation without the full support and understanding of top management and your colleagues. If you want to have a fighting chance for success, you may have to get commitments before you come aboard for staffing changes, additional staff, equipment, space, policy change authority, and time to turn things around. Clearly, none of *our* successors would have to face the challenge I just described!

81

PLAN YOUR WORK AND WORK YOUR PLAN

Among our most important personal assets as executives and would-be executives is our time and concentration. However, various events cause difficulties in being able to focus both of these resources in the most effective manner—real emergencies, unexpected interruptions—calls, issues, people dropping in, longer discussions than anticipated, cancellations, or foul-ups.

If we are to achieve maximum effectiveness in achieveing goals and objectives, we need the time and concentration to focus, in a laserlike way, on what we want to accomplish. Therefore, you need to carefully plan your time and effort—in essence plan your work.

This type of planning would involve setting forth specific goals and tasks for the year, quarter, month, week, and day. The longer the time period, the more general the plan can be and the specific assignment can be broader (e.g., to be accomplished in a particular month or last half of a month). But as one narrows to a month and week, and, of course, a day, the more specific and detailed the tasks and time period should be. You should block out in detail goals and tasks for the week and then in great detail and at specific times the agenda/schedule for each day. Time should be left free for unexpected events and also for just thinking and as a contingency. Logical groupings should be made so that instead of seeing Joe and Sally at three different times in a day or week, try to do everything in one shot, saving you and them time. Too often, we are interrupted in our concentration or in dealing with linked issues by having a helter-skelter appointment or meeting schedule. Related groupings can help improve discussions, time allocation, and decisions.

In carefully focusing on time and concentration, you will need to be tough. That is, some calls or appointments may have to be delayed so that your priorities can be met, or you may decide not to have appointments or take telephone calls during certain periods of a day or week so you can deal with your priorities (of course, true emergencies will have to be dealt with).

Once your plan of action is in place, what you will do, when, how, with whom, with what results, you need to make sure that you work your plan. You need to stick to your plan, to keep your attention on it, and as far as humanly possible, to avoid digressions, substitutions, delays. Whether you use lists, calendars, electronic devices or whatever, the objective is to have an ambitious but realistic plan of action for use of your time and energy, to seek ways, working with your staff, to provide the means to accomplish these goals and to work very hard on keeping the focus on what needs to be done. Those who are most successful in planning their work and working their plan are very likely to become and remain the leaders in the organization, while at the same time appearing to have time to spare.

82

LESSONS FOR AMERICAN MANAGEMENT FROM FEMALE-DOMINATED ORGANIZATIONS

Do we need to look across the ocean to Japan for ideas and techniques that will improve American management, or do we need only look across the street, city, state, or region to learn from female-dominated U.S. organizations? My recent experience in such an American organization, where the president and the majority of its senior executives are female, suggests that the latter may offer the answers we seek. Indeed, if what I sense is true, it may be described as an evolution of McGregor's human relations approach of Theory X and Theory Y and Ouchi's Japanese management approach Theory Z, to Theory F—a female-dominated organizational approach whose focus is on the individual and personal fulfillment, which results in greater organizational effectiveness and better bottom-line results.

Admittedly, the management style I have found in the female-dominated organization in which I work is not exclusive to such organizations. But there are significant differences in managerial style between this organization and other, male-dominated organizations for which I have worked. And a small survey of vice presidents of administration and finance at a few private women's colleges suggests some commonality in style among female-dominated organizations. Certainly there is sufficient evidence for further study and discussion.

The common characteristics or strengths I identified and found some support for were:

- More emphasis on collaborative decision making.
- Less concern with title and formal authority, more concern with responsibility and responsiveness.

- Less concern for empire building, power, domination, and consciousness about one's "turf."
- A greater concern with process and fairness.
- More decentralization.
- More democratic, participative, consultative management; less autocratic, domineering, ego-involved management.
- More concern with quality of outcomes.
- A greater responsiveness and concern for individual feelings, ideas, opinions, ambitions, and on- and off-the-job satisfactions.
- Generally more friendliness and openness in internal and external dealings.
- High value placed on loyalty, longevity, and interpersonal skills.
- More emphasis on skills as a listener and conversationalist.

Are these factors more likely to be found in female-dominated organizations than male-dominated ones? Maybe the issue is really irrelevant except from a theoretical basis. The key point may be that these characteristics should be evident in all U.S. organizations, regardless of their top management composition. The combination of these factors leads to an individual employee feeling very much valued by the organization, strongly connected to it and the individuals in and served by it. The employee considers himself or herself a significant member of a vital community that is concerned about his or her totality as a person as well as a contributor to the community or organization—and that seeks to provide a maximum sense of personal and professional fulfillment. This sense of community membership unleashes the individual's full creativity, productivity, and dedication.

83

ADVICE FOR WOMEN—HOW TO BREAK THROUGH THE GLASS CEILING

A fact sheet issued by NOW Legal Defense and Education Fund based largely on the Glass Ceiling Commission report "Good for Business: Making Full Use of the Nation's Human Capital" (1995) indicated:

1. "Although white men are 33% of the population and 43% of the work force, they hold 95–97% of senior management jobs and are approximately 60% of tenured professors, 91% of federal judges, 89% of the U.S. House of Representatives, 92% of the U.S. Senate, 99.8% of Fortune 1000 CEOs . . ."

2. "Women are 45.6% of the workforce and hold 43% of managerial jobs and 53% of professional jobs at all levels. Among executive vice presidents of business, only 9% are women. White women hold nearly 40% of middle management jobs while black women hold about 5 percent."

3. "In 1994, 52% of Fortune 500 companies had at least one woman on their boards of directors. In these companies overall, women held only 6.9% of directorships. However, less than 10% of the Fortune 1500 companies' boards of directors have women."

4. According to the Glass Ceiling Commission, "equally qualified and similarly situated citizens (in the private sector) are being denied access to advancement into senior-level management on the basis of gender . . . ."

5. "The Glass Ceiling Commission found that a major reason for women quitting their jobs is lack of career growth opportunities and dissatisfaction with their rate of progress."

6. But there has been progress as seen, for example, in figures for the legal profession.

	1960 (%)	1990 (%)
Law Students	3	41
Law Professors (tenured)	0.5	16.0 (1989)
Lawyers	3.5	21.6 (1993)
Federal Judges (Article III)	0.8	9

There are changes underway and promotional opportunities and the highest rung of the executive ladder will be more accessible for more women in the future than in the past. They will not have to be absolute super stars but have the same level of competence as males who achieve major positions. The climate is changing and men in their 20s and 30s are far more accustomed to women in large numbers in their classes, in leadership positions in college, as colleagues, and as supervisors in organizations than men in their 50s and 60s.

But while things may be much better for their daughters and better for their younger sisters, the talented, ambitious woman currently in business, industry, or virtually any organization needs to be able to break through a perceived glass ceiling, which may indeed be a real one. How can this be done? It requires actions under an individual woman's control as well as factors and forces beyond her control.

First of all, the company's leadership and culture needs to support the idea of equal opportunities in hiring, assignments, training, career development, and promotion for both sexes (and indeed for all individuals). The board, the chief executive, the chief operating officer, should demonstrate their real concern and commitment to this objective. By their commitment, it will be clear to executives and supervisors at all levels that equal opportunity for women is important to the company and to their supervisors and thus should be important to them. A president of a company who mentions to his or her vice presidents that there are very few women at significant executive levels and a board chairman/CEO who mentions to a president that there are few or no female vice presidents can help bring about actions in this regard. It might, on occasion, be necessary for staff members to remind those in authority of those facts, in case they haven't noticed or communicated.

Aside from depending on the initiative, wisdom, and good intentions of others, a woman should seek to break through the ceiling as a result of her own initiative and careful planning. Look for a mentor, or a champion, male or female, who can help you, guide you, create opportunities for you. You may wonder, what's in it for him (and in most cases it will be him, until there are more women in authority). Believe it or not, many executives like to mentor/champion people and for some there would be a "two-fer," a feeling of helping a bright young person move up, and of helping an underrepresented group join the executive or top executive tier. In today's executive world, individuals tend to work in teams rather than the traditional hierarchical model, thus finding a mentor or champion may be difficult. But the good and valuable team player can also be championed.

Networking is of particular value. Network with women in the company who are several rungs up and network with other women in the same industry and locale. The "young girl network" has to become as powerful as the "old boy network."

Strive to be noticed. Work as hard and as creatively as you can, be as involved as you can in the totality of company life. Volunteer for committees, extra assignments. In short, make it very hard for others not to recognize your ability and commitment. Get all the training and education available to you; acquire, if possible, skills, experiences and training that few women usually have compared with men so that you can demonstrate that your experience and skills are similar or superior to the males you are competing with for selection and promotion. If few women in the company or industry or in general, have manufacturing and production experience and skills, seek to acquire them so that you will stand out among women and also among men. If language skills and knowledge of international business seem to be the wave of the future for your company and industry, seek to acquire the knowledge, assignments, skills ahead of others. It's OK to use the fact that there are few women at a certain level and you are one of the few in the company and industry who have a particular set of skills and thus it would be good for the company and you if you were recognized by being promoted to a position that breaks through the ceiling.

I'm not sure that one can prove that women are more understanding, warmer, better at interpersonal relations, more sensitive to people's feelings than men, but there seems to be fairly common perception that they are. Don't be afraid to capitalize on the perception and play up your skills in those areas. At the same time, you need to overcome the perception that women aren't as "tough" or as "decisive" as men or are overly emotional by demonstrating that you can make the hard, tough choices unemotionally but perhaps in a more humane and caring way, which is just as, or even more effective than the "male model."

When women first began to enter executive training programs and the executive ranks in appreciable numbers, they wanted to blend in as much as possible. So they adapted to the "male" way of doing things. Even in their dress, they wanted to look like their male counterparts—the two- or three-piece blue or grey suit, solid or striped. But over time, as women have asserted themselves and proven their capabilities and that their own model, the "female way of doing things," is also appropriate and successful, dresses have appeared appropriate, albeit, sometimes with a jacket over the dress! The point here is that women need to balance the suit with the dress approach both literally and figuratively—both approaches are needed and valuable.

Choosing your industry and field can be helpful in terms of advancement opportunities. Certain fields (e.g., fund-raising) have a significant number of women in them and thus the glass ceiling is more likely to have been smashed than in other fields or in other industries. The not-for-profit sector has also, in general, been more hospitable to women and high-ranking women than, in general, the profit sector.

You need to be realistic in viewing your organization and industry. If no one has broken through the ceiling, do you think it is likely you will? You need to be willing to take risks and to be willing to change jobs and industries so be careful to avoid staying too long in one position or place if you are not making significant progress. Timing is of crucial importance—where you are, at what time, can determine whether you break through or not. You might consider more seriously than male counterparts taking positions with start-up companies or those in turnaround situations because of the potential (and risk) these hold.

Other points you might keep in mind:

- Involvements outside the organization in professional, civic and community affairs can give you valuable experience, knowledge, contacts, exposure, and notice that can help you internally and in your field.
- You'll need to be strong and confident, unintimidated by insecure or threatened supervisors.
- You'll need to earn respect and once you have it, particularly from major customers or clients, you are well on your way.
- Recruiting, training, developing, motivating your staff is of vital importance—if you can produce a highly qualified and motivated staff, you will be noticed because the major asset anyone on the rise has, in addition to his or her own qualities, is the quality and motivation levels of subordinates.

The preceding has been a bit of a "how-to" approach. The bottom line, though, is you have to be yourself. A good friend of mine, a woman who had broken through the glass ceiling as demonstrated by her position as a senior vice president of a major bank with major line responsibilities, decided, at age 47, to give up the prestige, power, compensation, and perks to pursue a lifelong dream to get a PhD, and to teach and consult. You have to be true to yourself.

In making a run for the top positions in an organization, a woman must recognize the price she (more likely than a male) may be asked to pay. The issue is career versus family. Although males are sharing the responsibilities of child rearing and maintaining a household to a more significant degree than in the past, and "Mr. Mom" captures attention, the burden of being the primary caregiver for the children still falls generally on women. Even the woman who seeks to balance career and children, either singly or with a male, knows that the time given up to childbirth and perhaps months or years to take care of an infant and young child are years where in most cases she is falling behind in the race with male and female competitors. Certainly, a company's actions toward both females and males concerning family leave, child-care programs, a generous maternity/paternity leave policy, a sick leave policy that takes into account an ill child (and by the way, an ill aged parent also places a disproportionate burden on women compared with men) all can help provide opportunities to balance career and family.

Some women when asked the question, "How can women break through the glass ceiling," respond, "They can't." They say the odds are stacked against them, particularly in the corporate world. Only the rare superstars, or the daughter or relative of the owner or powerful individual on the board or the CEO can break through because male dominance prevails and people tend to relate best to those who look and act and have similar experiences to themselves.

There is some validity to the view expressed. But there has been marked progress over the past two decades. Even though the progress may seem slow, there is reason for optimism. High competence is needed in all societies and in all organizations more today and in the foreseeable future than ever before. Competence not gender (or race or disability or sexual orientation) will have to be the deciding factor in gaining the executive suite, and finally, the largest office in the executive suite. It will take time and effort. We need as a society to move more quickly, but the momentum is there. The glass ceiling will be raised so that women climb higher, it will be dented, it will be broken!

84

How to Spell Relief—Alleviating Job Stress Caused by Organizations and Executives

Countless lectures, courses, articles, books, tapes, and programs are available to help executives manage stress caused by their job responsibilities. While managers focus on handling their personal stress, they should also be concerned about the health and well-being of their subordinates and colleagues. Executives are often unaware that their actions are inadvertently causing stress for subordinates, and they may want to do some soul searching to determine whether they and their organizations are practicing these stress-inducing activities. If so, they should change or modify their current practices to reduce stress on their employees.

Stress from one's job comes about because of problems within the following categories:

- Stress caused by the organization, including external and internal forces and factors acting on the organization and its division, departments, or units; the organization's culture; and the organizational and policy framework for the organization and for the particular unit.
- "Boss stress," including the boss's managerial style and personality.

ORGANIZATIONAL STRESS

External and internal forces and factors cause uncertainty about what will happen to the company, department, and individual. Even uncertainty about potentially positive things causes concern and stress. External forces may include possible, probable, or announced changes in products or services; orders and contracts; governmental funding and regulations; fixed expenses; competition from other organizations; reputation; and costs for employee benefits, equipment, energy, physical plant, or insurance.

Within the institution, factors may include the existing leadership; changes in leadership, organization, or environment; policies and practices; morale; goals and objectives; compensation; evaluations; and recognized unmet needs that may cost considerable sums. Other possible forces are conflicts between ethical standards and job demands and union-management disagreements. Because of a combination of external and internal factors, employees may become concerned about financial exigency or the need for deep expenditure reductions that raise issues of phaseout or elimination of functions, units, and positions; change in the fundamental nature of the institution; and merger with another institution.

Organizational Climate

The style of the organization, its tone, its priorities, and its concern for individuals may cause tension and anxiety. The culture may reward cooperativeness and teamwork among individuals or departments, or it may recognize and reward—in practice if not in statements—competition, protecting oneself, secrecy, and one-upsmanship. A lack of concern for personal crises, adequate compensation, stimulation, family and personal matters, and need for challenge all can create significant stress for the individual. Poor, outdated, or nonexistent policies and an inadequate communications system are two major factors in causing employee stress at all levels. Other elements include a lack of personal and professional growth or advancement opportunities, unsafe and/or unattractive working conditions and environment, excessive overtime requirements, and problems of boredom or burnout.

Organizational Framework

Depending on the organizational history and the individuals involved, the following may create undue problems for employees:

- Too many or too few levels.
- Too much or too little hierarchy.
- Too little (and less frequently too much) clear communication, and too few channels of communication—downward, upward, and laterally—particularly in regard to job responsibilities, authority, objectives, results, and problems.
- Illogical, time-consuming, and problem-producing grouping and assignment functions.
- Nonexistent or inadequate human resources management and general policies.

- Inadequate allocation of resources to meet goals and responsibilities.
- Inadequate formal and informal authority commensurate with responsibilities and objectives assigned.
- Unclear reporting relationships.
- Ineffective job placement.

BOSS STRESS

The following are frequent causes of problems arising from the boss's management style:

- Giving unclear assignments.
- Letting the subordinate be the "fall guy" when the boss or the organization is at fault.
- Giving too little or too much supervision.
- Providing too little or too much delegation.
- Playing favorites.
- Providing unclear or constantly changing work requirements.
- Being too soft or too hard on staff and other departments.
- Undergoing frequent changes in mood, style, and priorities.
- Withholding information so that subordinates don't have a clear picture of the entire project or problem.
- Failing to inform the individual on a timely and reasonably frequent basis of what's right or wrong with his or her performance and what corrective actions are necessary. It may be too late at the annual evaluation.
- Discouraging frankness, openness, and independent or creative thinking.
- Treating the individual as a child or robot rather than as a mature thinking adult.
- Neglecting to provide authority and rewards commensurate with responsibilities and performance.

- Failing to deliver on promises or agreements.
- Acting inconsistently.
- Failing to fight to maintain or increase a unit's budget, space, staff, scope, or authority.
- Hogging credit for himself or herself rather than recognizing contributions of subordinates.
- Neglecting to recognize individual needs of staff.
- Failing to praise a job well done or cheapening recognition by lavishly praising the ordinary.
- Refusing, when needed, to get his or her "hands dirty," or work overtime.

The Boss's Personality

Chemistry between individuals varies and can change over time, but the following aspects of a boss's personality are warning signs that problems are possible:

- Being indecisive.
- Shirking from making decisions, letting tasks pile up with hopes they'll go away, or making decisions when others should make them.
- Forcing others to take action because he or she refuses to do so on a timely basis, blaming others for failures, and taking credit if actions are successful.
- Being overemotional or, conversely, too laid back.
- Nitpicking to a high degree.
- Failing to trust individuals or credit them with any intelligence or creativity.
- Demeaning others.
- Demanding too much in too tight a time span (or demanding too little).
- Neglecting to provide clear instructions, guidelines, priorities, or deadlines.

- Failing to back up a subordinate who is under attack or, if the boss is under attack, blaming the subordinate.

- Lacking concern about the individual's work environment, stress, problems, and needs.

- Being too serious or too lighthearted.

- Having a perceived bias toward or against women, minorities, the disabled, or those who are different in some way, including such things as their weight or height or where they went to college.

- Failing to allow the individual to have a sense of personal accomplishment and trying to use the person as a robot rather than as a thinking human being.

- Being unworthy of respect—the boss's performance, motivation, interpersonal skills, or ethical standards may be low or may be lower than what he or she claims.

Each of these factors can cause mild to acute stress for individuals and several factors from one or more categories may be operating at one time.

Some actions that can be taken to alleviate or confront stress include:

- Reviewing the organization structure to logically group functions, clarify reporting relationships, and reduce delays in decision making and implementation.

- Improving upward, downward, and sideways communications with particular emphasis on clarity of responsibilities, authority, objectives, and deadlines.

- Developing a policies and practices handbook and reviewing material periodically.

- Emphasizing performance evaluation as both evaluative and developmental.

- Encouraging the human resources department to provide career management counseling and general counseling as well as advice and counseling in regard to an individual's supervisory or personnel problems.

The organization should discuss with all executives the aspects of personality and style listed in this chapter that might create stress for their subordinates and colleagues. The chief executive—whose support of this "attack on stress" is vital—or chief human resources professional should urge all executives to consider whether they are "guilty" of the "crimes" listed and encourage the executives to take actions to overcome or negate these points. Employees should be encouraged to ask their supervisors to work with them in overcoming or reducing these stressors. The chief executive and the human resources director should prepare executives at all levels to be receptive to these kinds of messages and not "kill the messenger" or attack the subordinate who is trying to improve working conditions. Just as the executive may hear some sensitive things about himself or herself from a subordinate, with the right groundwork and climate, the employee would be freer to speak to his or her superior, thus realizing the personal, professional, and organization benefits cited.

These actions would not only result in a significant reduction in stress but also an increase in job satisfaction and motivation and probably in productivity and performance. Further, turnover, burnout, illness, and absenteeism due directly or indirectly to stress would probably decline. A serious review of organizational and individual actions that cause stress and carefully thought-out and sustained efforts to take corrective action are well worth the effort.

85

FACTORS IN JOB SATISFACTION: PROBLEMS, POLICIES, PEOPLE, PLACE

A major concern of top executives is their employees' level of job satisfaction. Of particular interest is the job satisfaction of a manager's best people and people who have been identified as potential top-level executives. They generally need high job satisfaction and are likely to be concerned when their job loses its challenge or becomes boring. These people probably will seek new opportunities both within and outside the organization once job satisfaction begins to decline; if they stay, their dedication and performance may suffer.

The essence of providing job satisfaction is based on the problems individuals deal with or work on, the policies under which they work, the people with whom they work, and the kind of place where they work.

PROBLEMS

People need to face a variety of challenges that provide the opportunity to apply current—and develop new—knowledge and skills. An employee should be able to look back on past efforts and look forward to future efforts with a sense that he or she has obtained and will acquire more experience, skill, and knowledge in existing areas of expertise as well as the ability to develop new areas of expertise.

The astute manager will seek to provide a mixture of different kinds of assignments and challenges. Some assignments may be humdrum, but there should be enough challenges to provide the spark and the sizzle that can lead to job satisfaction. If their workload is mundane too often, employees will quickly become dissatisfied.

The effective manager must minimize the number of problems on the job, such as inadequate resources, unreasonable deadlines, and excessive red tape. The goal is to have as few negative challenges as possible. A good manager has to carefully monitor issues of organization, workload, deadlines, and resources.

POLICIES

An employee may face challenging assignments, but each employee needs to have the sense that the institution's policies, practices, and procedures enable people to accomplish their tasks and that management recognizes and rewards achievement and individual needs. Of major concern to top executives are clarity of organization and objectives; assignment of responsibility and authority; and policies and systems for resource allocation, accountability, control, planning and decision making, as well as for performance evaluation, compensation, promotion, employee benefit needs and personnel problems—for how things should operate, be communicated, and evaluated—in effect, management style and philosophy.

The concerned manager should review existing policies in all areas and focus on the need for policies that enable the individual and the organization to achieve objectives and to flourish while maintaining adequate controls, guidelines, accountability, and the degree of conformity necessary.

PEOPLE

Co-workers are as important to job satisfaction as are an institution's policies. Employees may face challenging assignments, but if they can't stand their colleagues, they are bound to become dissatisfied with their jobs. The professional competence and personal style, personality, attributes, and character of those with whom employees interact influence their sense of satisfaction.

Inevitably, there will be some imbalance between satisfaction with people and assignments, but executives must try to even the balance as much as possible.

The manager should work with employees and provide opportunities for training and discussions so that they can enhance their skills in working with others. A good manager will ensure that opportunities are created for building interpersonal relations, such as informal lunches and social events, and that mechanisms and channels exist to deal with disagreements, disputes, and dissatisfaction. Feeling comfortable and happy with colleagues is of great importance to job satisfaction. The more an employee feels that the unit (organization) is a caring place, the greater the chances for satisfaction. An observant manager will be people oriented in communications, actions, tone, and policies, and should recruit, reward, and promote individuals who demonstrate concern and skills in regard to interpersonal relations.

PLACE

The culture and climate of an organization are of considerable importance in shaping job satisfaction. Is there a sincere concern for people as well as productivity? Is there a sense of high standards of professional and personal conduct and of reasonable yet high expectations? Is there a real commitment to equal opportunity and affirmative action in hiring, assignments, promotions, and recognition? Are there explicit and strong policies on sexual and other types of harassment? Is there a sense of optimism, confidence, and pride about the organization and its people? Are the procedures and policies reasonably fair, intelligent, nonbureaucratic, and relatively hassle free? Is the institution considered a good employer, good at what it does, a good neighbor in the community?

In addition to these important considerations, there are the basic matters of whether the physical work environment is clean, safe, and attractive and whether various work amenities (e.g., parking, dining, exercise facilities, child care) are available at reasonable access and cost. Top executives can define the culture, climate, and tone of the institution by what they say and do—by precept and practice—thereby creating the type of organization that enhances job satisfaction.

A great portion of our waking hours are spent at work. Job satisfaction and the results achieved depend on how individuals react to the problems, policies, people, and place, and the actions top management takes to recognize and emphasize greater individual, unit, and organizationwide job satisfaction.

86

ASSESSING EXECUTIVE PERFORMANCE— THE CONSTRUCTION ANALOGY

Increasingly, boards of directors and chief executive officers are concerned about assessing their chief financial, operations, or administrative officers' performance and evaluating candidates for those positions when they become vacant. The complexity, difficulty, and broad scope of the most senior positions in meeting the organization's many external and internal issues and problems necessitates superior performance to successfully carry out responsibilities. This chapter seeks to capture the essence of a senior executive's job in an accurate and meaningful way in order to assist such officers in assessing their own performance and in developing goals for emphasis and improvement. This approach also might be helpful to presidents and boards in assessing performance and interviewing candidates for senior positions. And, indeed, the approach can be applied to presidents!

The components of a vice president's/senior vice president's responsibilities are analogous to the decision to erect a major new building, plant, or complex of buildings and the process of bringing that structure to completion and successful continuing operation. The outstanding executive plays five major roles: planner, architect, engineer, construction manager, and facilities director.

Other ways to describe a vice president's responsibilities are:

1. *In terms of Activities or Functions.* Their relationships with presidents, boards, external groups, other internal offices, subordinates, unions, vendors, customers and their functions in financial management, administrative management, planning, general management, and leadership.

2. *In Functional Terms.* Planning, organizing, staffing, deciding, budgeting, innovating, communicating, representing, controlling, and directing.

3. *In Terms of Mintzberg's Ten Basic Managerial Roles.* Figurehead, leader, liaison, news center, disseminator, spokesperson, entrepreneur, disturbance handler, resource allocator, and negotiator.

PLANNER

In building a major structure, one needs the skills of the planner-developer. The planner is the critical person in deciding:

- What is needed.
- Why it is needed.
- The goals and purposes of the structure.
- The building's location and relation to other structures of the organization.
- How the physical structure will meet immediate-, short-, and long-run operational, financial, and human resources concerns and needs.

The planner develops the financing and marketing plans and is concerned about the distinctiveness and competitiveness of the project.

A vice president fulfills the planner-developer role by dealing with similar issues for the organization.

Instead of structure, he or she is concerned about the organization and the various constituencies of the vice president and the organization.

ARCHITECT

The next role, both in building a structure and an organization is that of the architect. He or she takes the planner's ideas and concepts and translates them into a specific site and design to meet the needs of today and the future. The architect is concerned about what meets the eye—the look and feel of the building, the aesthetics, and the tone. Equally important, the architect designs the building to operate effectively and efficiently to meet the goals of the organization and the needs of its staff.

The vice president as architect translates the plan and vision into a sound operating organization concerned with:

- Appropriate governance and organization structure.
- Concrete plans, goals, and objectives based on the overall plan.
- The recruitment and retention of high-quality administrators and staff.

As architect, he or she seeks to shape the image of the organization, its climate and culture, its sense of community, and its confidence in itself.

ENGINEER

The engineer aspect of executive responsibility often is not stressed enough. In constructing a building, the contributions of the structural, mechanical, and electrical engineers are of critical importance in ensuring that the building is safe and that the various mechanical and electrical systems are cost-effective and reliable. The engineer ensures that the infrastructure of the building is sound and efficient.

The engineer aspect of an executive's role is also of critical importance. The master plan for the organization may be elegant and powerful, and the organizational structure and objectives may be strong and clear, but the infrastructure must be of at least the same high quality if the work of the planner and architect is to be effective and lasting. Thus, an eye for detail and a concern for the end results and for laying a solid foundation to weather turbulent times becomes the task of the vice president/engineer. This task is expressed in the policies and procedures of the organization, its style, and its concern for people and quality.

CONSTRUCTION MANAGER

The building has been designed, but now it must be erected using quality materials and craftsmanship according to specifications, on time, and within budget. This is the role of the construction manager.

The construction manager vice presidential role is related to the engineer's task but goes beyond to be concerned with present and future bottom-line results. He or she asks:

- Is the organization meeting its objectives and milestones on time, within budget, and with concern for quality and craftsmanship?
- Are major and minor issues being resolved on schedule?
- Are the details carefully checked out?
- Do things fit together?
- Have worst case issues been anticipated?
- Is the institution prepared to react to emergencies and unexpected events?

FACILITIES DIRECTOR

Finally, the building has been erected. Now it must be run, day after day, effectively and efficiently. Emergencies and day-to-day problems must be met and routine and special maintenance and cleaning must be planned and executed. These matters are the responsibility of the facilities director.

The facilities director aspect of the vice president's position is concerned with creating a system that provides timely information about day-to-day operations of the organization. The system should give early warning about deviations from plan; potential problems involving the organization's constituencies that may create poor public, governmental, or community relations; and opportunities for making "good things" happen. He or she must be concerned about mundane as well as major matters, for no matter how beautiful and sound the building, organization, or plan, the final test is the effectiveness and efficiency of operations and the foundation that is being set for the future.

MAKING THE GRADE

What separates the superb executive from the competent or above-average one, in my judgment, is his or her "grade" in each of the five categories.

Just as election to Phi Beta Kappa occurs for a very small percentage of students, so too only a small percentage of vice presidents would be inducted in to the Phi Beta Kappa society of vice presidential performance. They would have to attain an "A" in at least three of the five roles and no lower than a "B" or "B+" in the other two to have the minimum grade point average.

One would often assume that the "A" or "A+" must be achieved in the planner and architect roles and a "B" or "B+" would suffice in the engineer, construction manager, and facilities director roles. This assumption has some validity but need not necessarily be true. The specific strengths needed will vary depending on the organization's needs at a particular time in its history. An organization may indeed have had the right mix of strengths for a number of years in its vice presidency, but the demands of the job may change appreciably over time and the skills required may change. For some institutions, once the planner-architect's role has been largely fulfilled, it is more important that the vice president is very strong in the engineer, construction manager, and facilities director roles.

It is very rare, indeed unique, that an individual has the knowledge, skill, interest, time, and energy to achieve "A's" in all five of these extremely difficult roles. It is true, of course, that one can hire outstanding individuals at an assistant vice president level who have "A" skills and interests in the areas where the vice president is grade "B" or lower.

However, those who merit or aspire to induction in the vice presidential Phi Beta Kappa must attain the grades suggested to strengthen their organizations and lead them to greater heights. The Phi Beta Kappa vice president helps create, build, and maintain his or her organization. His or her goal is to achieve an institution that is planned and designed well and that meets its objectives effectively and efficiently while fulfilling the personal and professional goals and needs of the members of the organization's community and constituencies.

87

WORKING WITH A DIFFICULT PERSON

Unfortunately, there's no guarantee that your boss, colleagues, or subordinates will be good or easy people to work with. All of us hope and expect that our relationships on the job will be at least satisfactory. The more satisfactory they are, the better we feel. Job satisfaction is influenced to an important degree by how comfortable we feel with those with whom we are in frequent contact and indeed, how much or little we like them in their work capacities (their competence, fairness, style) and as individuals (personality and other attributes that make us like or dislike people). Some people stay or leave their positions primarily because of the organizational culture and climate rather than job content, compensation, challenge, or growth opportunities. A critical element in the climate is the quality of their personal and professional relationships. Looking forward to working with individuals and enjoyable lunchtimes, coffee breaks, and sometimes after-work social contacts can enhance the quality of work life considerably, as well as one's professional and personal life.

The flip side of the coin is working with difficult, disagreeable, or unpleasant people. The issue is how to deal with such people, assuming it is not an isolated incident or a particularly trying period in the individual's life. In many cases, the question becomes, How much are you able to adjust your thinking or style? How much can you stand? And there's a difference whether the difficulty is professional—his or her managerial style, competence, integrity—or his or her personal attributes—attitudes, harassment, prejudice, and so on.

The actions you might consider taking include discussing with the human resources department how you might deal with the problem or talking it through with your supervisor—indicate your concerns, what you can mutually do to improve things. If there are no results, you might consider going to your boss's supervisor, but this is a dangerous, last-resort step because it may very well exacerbate the situation with your superior. However, sometimes the higher official can help smooth things out or arrange a transfer. Finally, consider a transfer to another unit of the organization or seek other employment—this assumes that the situation is intolerable and the relationship cannot be improved. You might consider this when the stress and strain could be injurious to your physical or psychological health and your work performance. It is just not worth continuing the relationship because of the possible personal and/or professional impact on you.

For colleagues, the talking-through approach in regard to professional matters is recommended, with intercession, if necessary, by another colleague or your supervisor. If it is someone in another unit, your supervisor may have to get involved. The point to be raised is, "Your approach, position, style is creating a problem for me in accomplishing my work requirements and/or in our work relationship. How can we work together to modify, moderate, change the irritating condition?" The same approach can apply to colleagues on the same level in other units.

If it is the personal rather than work aspect, you should use whatever approach you feel comfortable with in indicating to someone that his or her actions cause you discomfort and dismay, and ask "How can we work this out?" You may also consider asking the human resources department to provide guidance and assistance or perhaps solicit help from a mutual friend. It may be that it cannot be worked out and you will just have to bear it, but at least you gave it a good try. You may even decide that working it out is so unlikely that you will have to bear it without mentioning it.

For subordinates, you as the supervisor are in a stronger position. Again, using the talking-through approach, if necessary with the help of the human resources department, is recommended. Here the approach would be indicating the aspect of the individual's professional behavior that is causing a problem and what you and the subordinate can do together to lessen/eliminate the problem. If counseling or training is required, the human resources department can be helpful.

You can follow up to see that there is improvement and if there is not, and in accordance with your organization's procedures, some disciplinary action might be necessary—warning, suspension, transfer to another unit, or request for resignation or discharge.

It is more difficult if personal styles or attributes are causing the problem. It is difficult if not impossible to change an adult's personality. Further, a perception that the supervisor is attacking the person rather than the individual's work performance can lead to considerable problems.

Here again, you would be wise to seek the human resources department's guidance, but if carefully thought out, you can approach the subordinate. You might say something like "Joe/Sally, we're all different and have different approaches/style, but I wonder if there's some way you can moderate/change/stop doing X, because it really makes me uncomfortable. It creates difficulties in my being able to deal with it, though I've been trying very hard." The matter may be so difficult or awkward to discuss or to change that you may have to just bear it as long as you can without discussing it. (Even after discussion and agreement for actions to be taken, it may still continue to exist.)

In essence, dealing with a difficult person requires you to think objectively and unemotionally whether the individual is indeed difficult or to what extent you or conditions beyond the individual's control are causing the difficulty. Further, is the situation difficult enough that you need to tackle it head-on in the ways previously suggested or through some adjustments and rethinking on your part? If it is a real and continuing difficulty, it is important for your own work performance, psychological well-being, and job satisfaction to meet the issue rather than avoid it.

88

CAN'T FIND A SOLUTION—SEEK TO BREAK OUT OF THE BOX

Every once in a while we end up stymied in seeking to solve a significant problem. Try as we might, applying all our technical knowledge and tools, experience, and inspiration, we still hit a dead end. In those instances, we may be trapped in the box of our usual and conventional thinking and approaches as are those with whom we consult in seeking solutions to long-standing complex problems or to new ones that have arisen and for which we seem to have no history and precedent to guide us.

As we seek to solve the problem or at least lessen its impact, we run into roadblocks in our own thinking and those of others. These roadblocks are suddenly erected or perhaps long-standing, blocking the usual highways we take to our designation. They are often expressed in such phrases as:

"We don't do it that way in this organization."

"We tried that before and it failed."

"We haven't got the resources—money, people, time, space, equipment."

"You'll be eaten alive by the boss (competition)."

"If it ain't broke, don't fix it."

"Be practical."

"You can lead a horse to water but you can't make him drink."

"You can't teach an old dog new tricks."

"Don't rock the boat."

"You can't change people."

"People don't want change."

"It isn't worth the trouble."

"Put it in writing."

"It's not in the budget."

"It's too off the wall."

"We've done well so far."

"It is not creative/new enough."

"You can't fight City Hall."

"A committee needs to look into that."

"I'll get back to you."

"Good idea—but it's not the right time."

What you need to do is determine how to dig under that roadblock, climb it, jump over it, go around it, or often better yet, take an entirely different road and thus avoid it. In short, break out of the box.

Another way to look at how boxed in we sometimes are can be seen in an exercise many of us have had to deal with. Until shown, we often get frustrated by our inability to solve this puzzle. We are asked to draw no more than four (often stated as three) straight lines through a set of nine dots so that these lines will cross through all nine dots, *without* lifting the pencil from the paper. (An example answer is on page 224.)

```
    •     •     •


    •     •     •


    •     •     •
```

The issue in this well-known puzzle is how to think outside the usual frame of reference, which in this example, literally and figuratively boxes us in.

An example from my own experience illustrates this tendency. At one institution, the faculty and staff were very upset and outspoken about the shortage of parking spaces in the college garage. The garage was very convenient underneath the center of the small urban campus and very inexpensive compared with parking in the neighborhood. But there were only 65 assigned spaces and a long waiting list, with individuals on the list for years. The shortage of space created deep concerns about the fairness of the system or lack of system of awarding spaces. The real issue, no matter how fair a system was devised, was essentially lack of supply of spaces to meet a legitimate need. An important constraint was that there was no space on campus to create a new garage or to expand the present garage (leaving aside the huge cost); though better layout of spaces and creating small car spaces might pick up about a 10% to 15% increase in spaces, what was needed was about a 90% to 100% increase. The solution to an important morale issue and one that tested the responsiveness of the administration was the formation of a committee of faculty and administration to think creatively. A fair and unanimously agreed-on system of awarding spaces was rather quickly devised as well as the idea of better layout and design of spaces, but that did not solve the fundamental problem—space for about 50 to 60 more individuals. The solution is not equivalent to rocket science or brain surgery, but it did take a bit of creativity, which seems so apparent in hindsight. We went to a system of valet parking with no assigned spaces, and thus were able to meet the need. People willingly paid somewhat more for parking, still well below neighborhood rates, and the problem was solved—we broke out of the box.

There are many approaches to think creatively. The essence, in my view, is as follows:

1. Seek to define, describe, simplify the problem.

2. Array as wide a range as possible of potential approaches and solutions, without criticizing any. Just list everything you and others can think of, the wild, the simple, just to get the thought out on paper or on a chalkboard.

3. Analyze, combine, synthesize, cobble parts of ideas together, discard . . . and then choose a few that seem best to focus on in great detail.

4. Choose the "best" solution. And, of course, implement.

In dealing with 3 and 4, you must force yourself to challenge assumptions, to probe and test, to visualize the future when the problem is solved, to use whatever techniques seem helpful to you and the group in "solving" the problem (e.g., idea swapping, creating metaphors, raising basic questions such as, "If there were no constraints on me of time, money, people, this is what I would do . . .") and then seek to adapt the ideal to the possible. Different settings, approaches, systems work for different people and different times. What is essential for those problems that don't lend themselves to your usual application of ideas, knowledge, and experience is to force yourself to think creatively, to question assumptions and the situation at hand and traditional ways of thinking and acting—the box that we are all in, almost all the time. And then through creativity and focus, you can break out of the box! It can be exhilarating!

The secret is to break out of the box formed by the dots. For example:

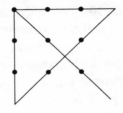

89

Manage Your Career—Don't Just Drift or Get Swept Along

It's quite interesting to delve into the paths taken in choosing and staying in a career. We go through college placement offices, answer a newspaper ad, work for a relative or friend of a relative, network, contact a placement agency, get contacted by a "headhunter," send out hundreds of resumes, get information from a friend, relative, or just fall into something, somehow.

Our thinking about careers, from early childhood on is shaped by the occupations and the reaction to their occupations of parents, relatives, parents and relatives of friends, neighbors, movies, television, books. We are further influenced by where we live, go to school, economic circumstances of family and friends, conditions in our neighborhood, region, and country. Often as a teenager and college student, we really don't know very much of the details of what it is really like to be a _____, or to spend 20 or 30 or 40 years working as a _____ or in the _____ industry. And we also have little knowledge about the wide range of jobs in society now and what are likely to be job growth areas and new jobs in the near and far term.

And many of us, even five or more years after beginning full-time employment, don't have a good understanding of who we are in terms of job and careers. Who am I, what do I want in life, what do I want out of a job or career are critically important questions that most of us do not ask. Or when we do ask, it usually happens when we have been fired, laid off, downsized, or had a physical or life calamity arise that makes us question our values, goals, and priorities.

Career planning and management, concern about your career should be a major focus of attention, not only at age 40 or 50, after being forced out of a job for one reason or another, or because of being bored or not excited/energized/interested in your present work and the outlook for the future. It is something that you should pay attention to beginning in your college years and perhaps even in high school, and continue to be interested in throughout your career. Even when you are delighted with your job and what the future seems to hold, you should be interested in actively managing your career; you cannot afford to be a passive investor or observer in your future.

Whether through career counseling, reading books, taking various tests such as the Myers-Briggs, Strong Interest Inventory, internships, talking with people in different lines of work, networking, keeping active in professional organizations, keeping in touch with executive search agencies—you need to be involved in thinking about and planning your career.

But first of all you need to know yourself. Aside from the tests previously mentioned and courses you can take, you can do a self-assessment. You need to answer the following questions truthfully:

1. What things make me happy that lie within the control of myself, things that lie within the control of others, or fate or circumstance?

2. What things make me unhappy that lie within the control of myself, things that lie within the control of others, or fate or circumstance?

3. List 12 things you regard as achievements, large or small, that you feel good about. Analyze why you feel good about them.

4. What values are really important to you? List and rate what you regard as negative job qualities—things that are personally distasteful (e.g., job is boring, has no security, pay is poor, working conditions poor, little recognition by others, work a lot alone, a lot of paperwork).

5. What kinds of work and nonwork activities do I really like or really dislike?

6. What are my real talents/skills and which of these are personally meaningful?

7. What latent or underdeveloped interests or talents would I want to make a real effort at developing?

8. Which of my values, interests, talents can best be met in a job and career?

9. Which of my values, interests, talents can best be met outside of work and a career?

10. How can I achieve a balance between work and nonwork activities to meet my most significant values, interests, and talents?

11. How important is work or career in contrast to the other elements in the following equation: Life = personal life, family + work/career + nonwork activities/interests?

12. List and rate what you regard as positive job qualities.

13. Rate yourself in regard to various aspects of decision-making skills (e.g., go about getting what I need to know, differentiate

between important and unimportant information, use information and apply it to a decision, be aware of my values and apply them to a decision, set clear objectives, develop alternatives and narrow them down, reach various possible outcomes, use a strategy for making critical decisions).

14. List the goals you want to accomplish, immediate, short, midterm, and long range in your career and life; analyze what could keep you from reaching these goals (don't have skills, ability, knowledge needed, don't want it badly enough to really work for it, afraid of failing, afraid of views of others, it's really too difficult). What can you do so that the negative things don't prevent you from reaching goals; who can help you? What are your chances for success and why do you feel that way? What are the good and bad things that might happen if you reach the goal? After reviewing all these factors and the chances that the good or bad things will happen, do you still want to try to reach the goal? If you still want to proceed, what are the immediate and continuing steps that must be taken? Assign yourself deadlines for taking and accomplishing each step.

The more you objectively understand yourself the better able you will be to analyze job opportunities and challenges. Some jobs and careers may just not be right for your values, skills, and style, and in reassessing your values, you may find yourself unable or unwilling to make the changes necessary to achieve success in a particular job and industry.

In terms of active career management, depending on your age and stage in your career, you need to assess the likely changes in your profession or industry, 5, 10, and more years ahead. This will enable you to take the necessary experiential, educational, and training steps and opportunities to become qualified for dealing successfully with the new and upcoming techniques, skills, style, and knowledge or to transfer your professional abilities to other industries and careers.

Career management is necessary at all stages of your career if you are to meet and perhaps even exceed your potential:

- Keep abreast of what's happening in your company, field, industry, and allied fields and what is happening in the economy, area, region, country, internationally, that may directly or indirectly affect you now or in the future.

- Understand the company's and industry's culture and see how that meshes with your values and style. There may not be a good fit.

- Seek ways to get noticed through the quality, quantity, and timeliness of your work product but also through your professional and personal style. Volunteer for assignments, get involved in community affairs, work on your interpersonal and communication skills.

- Network. Make contacts and keep in touch with peers and supervisors within your organization, industry, and in your geographic region. Sometimes an opportunity can arise not directly in your field but your skills may be transferable and you may have become known and respected through your community or professional involvements.

- If you have time, talent, and opportunity seek to write, lecture, or teach or be involved in professional organizations in your field as a way of keeping current and ahead, sharpening your knowledge and skills, and earning notice and respect for your views and accomplishments.

- When opportunities present themselves and in appropriate ways, let executive search agencies know about you, and let peers and supervisors know of your aspirations and accomplishments. Modesty is indeed a virtue but at times one can be overly modest.

It is important to remember that you and your career evolve over time; your values and aspirations change as your life experience increases. As the sign in a bar in a Western town stated—"I ain't what I ought to be and I ain't what I'm going to be . . . but I ain't what I was!"

Understand that the current and future career challenges are quite different from a generation ago. For many people, there is a significant expansion of the meaning of a successful career. The description of success goes beyond status, recognition, financial, and material criteria to include psychic income, achievement of life goals, self-actualization. There are increased and rising expectations of a more highly educated workforce as to what they want out of a career, and these expectations sometimes cross over to a sense of entitlement. As we go into an era of rightsizing, the lack of achievement of "entitlements" can produce strong feelings of disappointment, anger, depression.

There is increased concern for the totality of life—the balance of work, interests, and activities, nonwork interests and activities, a personal life, a family life—and work for many is not the largest factor in the equation and may well be the smallest. The increase of women in the workforce, and in executive roles, and in nontraditional occupations and roles has led to greater awareness of the needs of women and all employees (e.g., dual-career couples, single parents) in the areas of health and family concerns, day care, elder care, use of sick leave, family leave. The increasing diversity of the work force at all levels also poses new challenges—minorities, individuals with various disabilities, individuals not born in the United States or brought up in families where English is not the primary language who bring different cultural perspectives and language capabilities, individuals who have not had adequate education or training to deal with the competitive, technical environment of today and the future.

All of the preceding and related issues place a premium for career success and advancement on those who can do well in meeting the challenges of a workforce with different characteristics from those of preceding generations, and who feel differently about their jobs.

The theme throughout this discussion is that managing your career is as important, and perhaps more important, difficult, exciting, and rewarding than any other managerial task you will face. You may find it useful once a year, on New Year's Day, your birthday, your anniversary date in your organization, to assess where you have been, where you are, and where you are going. In total honesty, you should review and analyze the past year to determine what you have really accomplished. But more important, what new, enhanced, enriched, enlarged skills, abilities, knowledge have you acquired or are well along to acquiring that you didn't have last year? What solid achievements could you, in truth, add to your resumé, that would make you more valuable if you were looking for a job? You also need to "take your temperature" every year or two, to determine whether you are really happy with where you are going and what the future seems to hold. If your temperature is not good and you do not have anything meaningful to add to your resumé, you need to assess what you have to do to improve the prognosis. Although some people get boxed in or caught in the organization because of compensation, status, age, lack of opportunity elsewhere, feeling comfortable and not wanting to undertake new risks and challenges are more often the reasons for staying with a company. If retirement is not imminent, you need to look toward restoring challenge and zest to your career. This may involve new assignments, a lateral transfer, developing other interests, or leaving the organization and industry.

We all spend enough hours and weeks at work that striving for as great job satisfaction as possible is well worthwhile. Career management takes considerable time, effort, thought, introspection, planning and action, but in terms of both material and psychic criteria, it is probably the best investment you can ever make.

90

THE NEXT DECADE: AN EMPHASIS ON RIGHTSIZING, LINE OPERATIONS, TRADE, PEOPLE, PRODUCTIVITY, CREATIVITY, CUSTOMER ORIENTATION, AND INFORMATION

As we struggle with the problems of today and this year, it is worthwhile to get a sense of what the next 10 years are likely to bring so that we might prepare ourselves and our organizations. Each person who attempts to look ahead will probably list things differently, but I suggest that there will be increased emphasis on rightsizing, line operations, trade productivity, creativity, customer orientation, information, excellence, and people.

As indicated in a previous chapter, "rightsizing" is the current and future trend, but there is a need for concern about its goals, how it is done, the short- and long-range impact on the organization and on the people affected.

We have come to realize that our product design, manufacturing techniques, quality standards and controls, product functionality, marketing, and selling no longer enjoy a great competitive advantage in the increasingly competitive and international marketplace (a marketplace that will become even more competitive). In fact, the competition is such that American manufacturers will be under increasing pressure to manufacture products abroad. Our emphasis in recent years has been on the MBA holder who is trained in finance, but generally has little experience or desire to get involved in production problems, or even marketing, or sales. Now and in the future, we will place more emphasis on the various aspects of production, marketing, and sales, and people who have experience and capabilities in regard to the making, delivering, and selling of the basic products of the firm. The power will shift from staff functions to line functions with emphasis on customer satisfaction.

The current emphasis on international trade and selling U.S. products abroad will continue and become even more important. We will have to adapt American skills in marketing and production of products and services to the needs and attitudes of different culture, many that are quite different from our own. The emphasis on increasing our sales of goods and services to foreign customers will require us to become significantly more knowledgeable of foreign countries—their people, language, history, customs, culture, traditions, ways of doing business, government, and so on. This need will have an impact on education provided in our colleges and universities, business schools, professional schools, and also in the training provided by businesses to their employees. The globalization of the economy will have a profound impact on careers and career advancement and on education and training in the United States.

Coupled with this will be increased stress on productivity of machines, capital, and people. Technology will be emphasized, but so will improved policies, procedures, and practices to remove bottlenecks and increase output. Major concern will be devoted to motivation of staff so that human productivity is improved. Further-more, with the workforce changing to a primarily white-collar, ser-vice and "knowledge" workforce, increased concern will be shown to improving productivity in that sector (e.g., by analyzing how time can be used most effectively).

There will be increased stress on innovation and creativity in terms of new products and approaches or better ways to do what we've always done. Concern will be given to creating climates and better recognition and reward systems in which creativity can flourish.

There will be increasing emphasis on a customer orientation—how the organization can serve its customers and clients. A superior product will not be enough to capture leadership in one's field or in-dustry over a long period. What will be necessary, in addition, is a concern for meeting the customer's needs and concerns. Thus a sincere service orientation will be necessary—providing what is wanted, how, when, and where it is wanted, with reliable, consistent, outstanding service. Whether the product is a car, a watch, a suit, or a legal, accounting, or medical service, the customer will and should expect more in regard to quality and quantity of service and those who wish to do well will meet the customer need.

Information flow will be emphasized, including two-way commu-nications. Growing familiarization with computer technology and applications of computer technology will have a profound impact on most organizations. Fewer people will be required in general as will fewer supervisors and middle-level staff, particularly as com-puters can replace some of the functions of these groups. Comput-erization allows for a vast increase in the number of entrepreneurial units and profit centers, thereby reducing the number of individuals in middle management and permitting the change of the organiza-tional structure to a horizontal rather than a vertical structure. The increased information flow primarily through computerization will require greater emphasis and technological improvements in regard to safeguarding computer data.

There will be an increased concern about standards of excellence in all that is done, from the smallest task by the lowest person in the organization to the most complex, as performed by the president. The message of *In Search of Excellence** will be a valuable guide for achieving excellence. The book pointed out that the well-managed companies had the following characteristics: an action orientation— do it, fix it, try it; keep things simple and lean; emphasize the customer; improve productivity through people; encourage entrepreneurship through operational autonomy; place stress on a particular business value; do what you know best; maintain simultaneously both loose and tight controls.

Finally, and probably most important, we will have to look at how we treat people who interact with and within the organization. Our relations with customers, the public, vendors, and stockholders will become of more concern than in the past. Of great importance will be how we treat our peers and subordinates and all who work within the organization. We will need more skilled and motivated workers. We will need to build loyalty, dedication, and concern for highs standards of excellence in product and service. Competition will be strong internally in firms so that performance and personal relations will be of greater concern. The ability to motivate others and the polices and systems needed to support this motivation will be of increasing importance. There will need to be more of a sense of a team than of a hierarchy and the sense of flexibility and less rigid lines and status symbols between managers and workers. There will have to be a belief by employees at all levels that they are part of the organization, they are involved, important, and eligible for a "piece of the action." Thus, new approaches will be necessary in regard to rewards, recognition, compensation, and structure.

I have sketched some of the trends as I see them, but basic to all of them—rightsizing, customer orientation, trade, line operations, productivity, creativity, information, and excellence—is whether we will be successful in improving the way we view and deal with the people in the organization.

---

*Thomas J. Peters and Robert H. Waterman, Jr., *In Search of Excellence*. New York: Harper & Row, 1982.

CONCLUSION

———————— ⟫✕⟪ ————————

You now have 90 tools, suggestions, and concepts to help you get to the heart of good management. The Appendices will offer a way for you to modify the ideas presented as well as adding your own, based on your own experience and a way to apply them to personal life and nonwork situations. Although each idea can and should be used immediately and throughout your career, I offer a caution. Carefully study the particular situation before you apply the suggestion. This can be illustrated by what happened to a friend. He had a job offer that required him to move very quickly. He put his house up for sale at a low price for a quick sale. The good news is that he sold it in four days. The bad news is that he had not received the offer in writing and, thus, did not have a new job. In short, use the guidelines carefully; don't skip or jump them!

I have tried to indicate the challenge of excellent management and the exhilaration and personal and professional fulfillment one can achieve in striving for excellence. Good enough isn't good enough and this book attempts to convey a sense of the need for high standards and maximum effort for ourselves, our colleagues, our organizations, and society.

We need to go beyond concern as to whether Americans still have the same dedication to the work ethic as we supposedly had 30 or more years ago. Our concern should be whether we want to have a commitment to excellence and, if so, how we are to develop and maintain it. Such a commitment and action based on goals of excellence will come from the heart as well as the mind. Good intentions or uplifting rhetoric won't be enough. We must continuously learn, grow, and reach beyond our grasp as individuals and as organizations. We must strive to develop the fullest potential and expand the potential of ourselves, all members of the organization, and the organization itself. It will take considerable time, effort, and dedication, but

the rewards are more than equal to the demands placed on us. I
strongly urge you to commit and dedicate yourself, personally and
professionally, to pursue and strive for excellence in every way possible—to indeed have a passion to manage and live your job, career and
life at the highest level of excellence and achievement.

Appendix A

USING THIS BOOK FOR CONTINUED
SUCCESS, LEARNING, AND GROWTH

The reader might wish to keep a record of successful application of the ideas and learning derived and of new or modified guidelines that could be used in the future, based on the knowledge gained in particular situations.

Tables A.1 and A.2 are charts that may be helpful in maintaining this record and in developing your own management philosophy.

Table A.1. Ideas in the Book

Statement of Management Idea (Page Number)	When It Was Applied; Under What Circumstances; (Factors Considered in Applying It)	Results
1. _____	_____	
_____	_____	
2. _____	_____	
_____	_____	
3. _____	_____	
_____	_____	
4. _____	_____	
_____	_____	
5. _____	_____	
_____	_____	
6. _____	_____	
_____	_____	
7. _____	_____	
_____	_____	
8. _____	_____	
_____	_____	
9. _____	_____	
_____	_____	
10. _____	_____	
_____	_____	
11. _____	_____	
_____	_____	
12. _____	_____	
_____	_____	

Evaluation—Other Factors to Consider; Modifications Necessary—Why?	Restatement (If Necessary) of the Core Idea

Table A.2.   New Ideas

Statement of Management Idea	When Discovered Under What Circumstances	Factors to Consider in Application—How/When to Apply It
1. _____		
2. _____		
3. _____		
4. _____		
5. _____		
6. _____		
7. _____		
8. _____		
9. _____		
10. _____		
11. _____		
12. _____		

Evaluation—When Was It Applied; Under What Circumstances; What Were the Results?	*Modifications Necessary in Statement or Its Application*

Appendix B

MANAGEMENT GUIDELINES APPLIED TO PERSONAL LIFE AND SITUATIONS

Many of the guidelines can be applied beyond the workplace in dealing with spouses, significant others, children, parents, friends, and in the various situations, problems, opportunities that constitute the joys, stresses and strains of the totality of life. Each reader will bring to the guidelines the influence of his or her life experience and personality and will react, negatively or positively, to the application of the guidelines based on those factors. The following list matches some of the guidelines with their possible applications. Table B.1 is a chart that may be helpful in tracking your applications of the guidelines.

Guideline	*Application*
Management Style	
The Heart of the Matter	Success in relationships, success in interests, hobbies
Good Enough Isn't Good Enough	All aspects of life
The Complacency Trap	Striving to improve relationships and one's situation
Get Hot . . . Sometimes	Need to take risks, be creative, break out of the box
Treat Everyone Alike, but Not the Same	Dealing with children, loved ones, friends, acquaintances
Be Kind to Those Coming In and Going Out	Applies to the young and the old, new and old neighbors and friends
Resist Revenge	Relationships with family, friends, neighbors, rivals
Seeing and Believing	Personal relationships and situations

Guideline	*Application*

Management Style (Continued)

It Pays to Care	All aspects of life—for you as well as those who benefit from your caring
You've Gotta Believe	All relationships—or else, one becomes very hard and cynical
When You Knock on Your Door, Is There Anyone Home?	Developing yourself, know who you are and who you want to be
Grow a Reasonably Thick Skin	To avoid being too sensitive or emotional in nonwork personal and other situations, which can be harmful to you and to achieving your goals
Nobody's Perfect	Applies to you and everyone in all situations
Think before You Speak	All situations and relationships
Perceptions Are as Important as Reality	Personal situations, your children, spouse, others
You Can't Take It with You	Enjoy life
You've Gotta Pay Your Dues	Earning trust in relationships and in nonjob organizational involvement
Are You Paying Enough Psychic Income?	To family, friends, acquaintances, and those you deal with
Those Who Wear Well Succeed	All personal and organizational relationships
Look for Small Quick Victories	Applies to all situations where you seek to establish yourself, whether in nonwork organizational involvements, personal relationships, etc.
Watch Out for Being One Deep	When working on nonwork activities or in working through family matters

Management Skill

Where You Stand Depends on Where You Sit	Realize that you bring biases and perceptions to every situation—it's very hard, if not impossible to be "totally objective"
Success Comes to Those with a High Tolerance for Ambiguity and Frustration	Many situations and relationships are not as clear and uncomplicated as one might hope.

Guideline	*Application*
Management Skill (Continued)	
Know When You and Others Don't Know	It is difficult to admit that you or someone you love or respect just doesn't know or is wrong.
Evaluate Yourself and Others	You need to take your temperature once in a while and to honestly evaluate your (and others) strengths and weaknesses
Treat Trivialities Trivially, or Don't Sweat the Small Stuff	All relationships and situations— easier to say and think than to do— but it really pays off
It Takes More Time to Do Things Than You Hope but Less Time Than You Think	Your various activities and commitments
Control, but Don't Overcontrol	Dealing with nonadult children as well as others
Innovate or Vegetate	Seek to change ways of doing, thinking, building relationships to add zest to life
Decide, Damn It!	All situations and relationships except when, analytically, it is best not to decide.
Make Sure Your Base Is Solid before Expanding It	Before undertaking new responsibilities and commitments, make sure you're comfortable with what you already have
Don't Squander Your Most Important Resources—Time, Energy, Thought	Applies to all relationships and situations—except if squandering gives you pleasure!
The Bottom Line Is Critical—How You Got There Is Also Critical	You may strive for success in achievements, situations and relationships but what you had to do (or not do) or give up is of great importance
Can't Find a Solution—Seek to Break Out of the Box	At times, nontraditional thinking and approaches are needed in all aspects of life—problem solving, personal relationships, etc.

Table B.1. Applying Guidelines to Personal Life and Situations

Guideline	Application	Result
1.		
2.		
3.		
4.		
5.		
6.		
7.		
8.		
9.		
10.		
11.		
12.		

INDEX

About the Author

———— ⊱✦⊰ ————

Sigmund G. Ginsburg was appointed Senior Vice President for Finance and Business Development at the American Museum of Natural History in New York City on April 1, 1995. He also serves as Director of the Hayden Planetarium/North Side Project. He joined the Museum on December 1, 1994, as Vice President for Business Development. He had previously served as Vice President for Finance and Administration at Barnard College in New York City (1984–1994), Vice President for Finance and Treasurer of the University of Cincinnati in Cincinnati, Ohio (1978–1984), and as Vice President for Administration and Planning and Treasurer of Adelphi University in Garden City, New York (1972–1978).

He was Assistant City Administrator in the Office of the Mayor, City of New York (1967–1972) and was awarded the City of New York Merit Award in 1969. He was Founder and Director of the New York City Urban Fellowship Program (1969–1972), and served as Senior Management Consultant and Special Assistant to the Deputy Mayor in the Office of the Mayor (1966–1967). He has held positions with the Port Authority of New York and New Jersey, Hudson Institute, and the Office of the Secretary of Defense. He served as a lieutenant in the U.S. army and was awarded the Army Commendation Medal.

Mr. Ginsburg taught primarily graduate courses in management from 1967 to 1995 at Bernard Baruch College and John Jay College of City University of New York; Adelphi University; the University of Cincinnati, where he was Adjunct Professor of Business Administration and Adjunct Professor of Higher Education Administration, the New School for Social Research; and Fordham University. He has also lectured widely and consulted.

Mr. Ginsburg is the author of: *Ropes for Management Success: Climb Higher, Faster; Management: An Executive Perspective;* co-author of *Managing the Higher Education Enterprise* and editor of

Paving the Way for the 21st Century: The Human Factor in Higher Education Financial Management. He is the author of the chapter "Human Resources Management and Employee Relations" in *College and University Business Administration,* Fifth Edition, chapters in five other books, as well as 125 articles dealing with general, financial, and human resources management, higher education administration, and public administration. His articles have appeared in *Business Officer, The Public Interest, Columbia Journal of World Business, Public Administration Review, Educational Record, Inc., Glamour, Management Review, Personnel, American School & University, The President, AAHE Bulletin, Trusteeship, The Urban Lawyer, Supervisory Management, Facilities Manager, Personnel Journal,* and in Braniff Airline's in-flight magazine. He has appeared on radio and television programs discussing management problems and had a weekly radio program "The World of Work" in Cincinnati dealing with listeners' questions. He is listed in *Who's Who in America.* He served as a member of the Advisory Council of TIAA-CREF (Chairman 1994–1995). He serves on the Advisory Board of the New York City Urban Fellows Program, and the Board of Directors of Greenwich House, Inc.

He is a Phi Beta Kappa, magna cum laude graduate of Dartmouth College, where he held the highest honor the College bestows, the Daniel Webster National Scholarship, and was awarded the Colby Prize in Political Science. He did graduate work on a James B. Reynolds Fellowship at the London School of Economics and Political Science, and was a Littauer Fellow at Harvard University, where he earned the MPA degree. Mr. Ginsburg received the Neal O. Hines Publications Award in 1992 from the National Association of College and University Business Officers, and the first Award for Distinguished Service to the New York City Urban Fellows Program on its twenty-fifth anniversary in 1994.